JavaScript
for the Business Developer

S0-BZH-846

JavaScript
for the Business Developer

Mike Faust

MC | PRESS

MC Press Online, LP
Lewisville, TX

JavaScript for the Business Developer
Mike Faust

First Edition

First Printing—June 2007

MC Press offers excellent discounts on this book when ordered in quantity for bulk purchases or special sales, which may include custom covers and content particular to your business, training goals, marketing focus, and branding interest.

For information regarding permissions or special orders, please contact:
MC Press
Corporate Offices
125 N. Woodland Trail
Lewisville, TX 75077 USA

For information regarding sales and/or customer service, please contact:
MC Press
P.O. Box 4300
Big Sandy, TX 75755-4300 USA

ISBN-10: 1-58347-070-0
ISBN-13: 978-1-58347-070-1

12/07

Downloadable code is available at:
http:www.mcpressonline.com/mc/Forums/Reviews/5084

For Leslie, Jason, Alyssa, Chris, and Brandon.

You are my world.

Contents

Introduction

In this book, you'll explore the JavaScript language and how this powerful scripting language can be used to enhance your web pages. Beyond that, you'll explore JavaScript from a business programming perspective. The needs of the business programmer can differ greatly from those of a web page designer.

Chapter 1 focuses on the role that JavaScript can play in the business world. In chapter 2, you'll examine the origins of JavaScript itself, where it came from, what it is, and how to use it. Chapter 3 explains the language structure of JavaScript, including the syntax used, along with the objects, methods, and events supported by JavaScript. Chapter 4 covers the concept of cascading style sheets and explains the role that they play in JavaScript programming. In chapter 5, you examine simple JavaScript functions you can use in your own applications right away. These simple functions will get you started down the road to understanding how to build JavaScript functionality to build dynamic business applications. Chapter 6 takes you into the world of AJAX—no, not the cleaner, *Asynchronous JavaScript and XML*. This technology gives business programmers access to literally a whole new world of application tools. So that you don't have to key the code for the many examples in the book, you'll find a zip file with the companion code for this book at *http://www.mcpressonline.com/mc/Forums/Reviews/5084*.

When you've completed this book, you'll have a better understanding of how powerful the JavaScript language is. Along the way, you'll have some fun, too, creating useful and just plain cool applications. So sit back and fasten your seat belt; we're about to blast off into the world of JavaScript.

1

Getting Down to Business

As a business programmer, you might be thinking that JavaScript is only for web page programmers. But to paraphrase the old orange juice slogan, JavaScript's not just for web programmers anymore. JavaScript can help you create dynamic business applications using a web browser as the interface. In this chapter, you'll explore why JavaScript makes sense in the business programming world. You'll learn the "how" behind this in chapters to come.

The Interface

If you've worked with static HTML, or even server-side scripting technologies like ASP or PHP, you know that this technology tends to be very "flat"—once an HTML or ASP document has been loaded, it has to be reloaded, or submitted to a server, for its appearance to change. This is where JavaScript comes in. Using JavaScript functionality, you can easily turn standard web-browser output into a more dynamic and easier to use interface.

Creating a dynamic, user-friendly interface is one of the best arguments for using JavaScript when building business applications. An application can work great and offer bulletproof reliability, but if it has an awkward or outdated look and feel, users might avoid it altogether. Since the interface is what your users see, it really does play a huge role in their overall impression of the application, as well as affecting usability.

Consider an HTML page that displays the current date and time on the screen. With standard HTML, the date and time will only be updated when the page is reloaded. Using JavaScript, on the other hand, the information can be updated every second, giving the appearance of a digital clock. Here is the source to do that:

```
<TABLE ALIGN=CENTER BORDER=2 BGCOLOR=black>
    <TR>
      <TD ALIGN="CENTER" STYLE="COLOR:GREEN; WIDTH:250;" ID="Clock">
          <SCRIPT LANGUAGE="JavaScript">
              function showTime()
                {
                curTime = new Date();
                document.getElementById("Clock").innerHTML = curTime;
                setTimeout("showTime()", 1000);
                }
              showTime();
          </SCRIPT>
      </TD>
    </TR>
  </TABLE>
    </BODY>
</HTML>
```

This example embeds the JavaScript source directly inside of the table's <td> element. When the page is initially loaded, the showTime() function is called. It populates the table cell with the current date and time. As a last step, the setTimeout() method is called. It will call the showTime() function again in exactly 1,000 milliseconds (one second). Figure 1.1 shows the clock output, displayed in Internet Explorer 6.

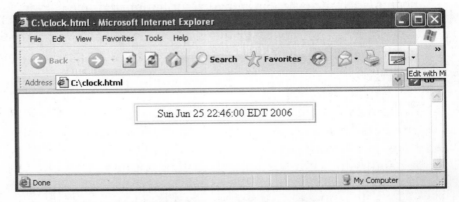

Figure 1.1: This dynamic digital clock is created with JavaScript.

This simple example illustrates JavaScript's ability to update data in real time, directly to the user interface. While this specific example just displays the system time, a similar technique could be used to obtain information from an XML web service and display the data to a browser, updating the information at specified time intervals. This technique could be further extended to do things like display up-to-the-minute stock market data, or monitor the status of a shipment.

The key here is that the browser display is updated without having to reload the page. Remember that the interface itself is generated by the web browser. This means that your application deployment becomes relatively simple, since every workstation in your office already has the required client application. JavaScript extends a web page's GUI interface by making it more dynamic and interactive.

Let's look at another example: an item-requirements web page. This application might display a list of items and the relevant quantity on order, quantity required, etc. Without JavaScript the user might have to click on the item-number field to display additional item information. This action would send a request to the server to retrieve the web page containing the item's information. Figure 1.2 shows the flow of this application.

While this approach would work quite well, it shows the disconnect between the client application and the server. Using JavaScript, this information can be included when the page is initially loaded, hidden from view until the user hovers the mouse over the item-number field. At that point, a box containing all of the item data can be displayed within the browser window. Figure 1.3 shows the flow that can be created using this method.

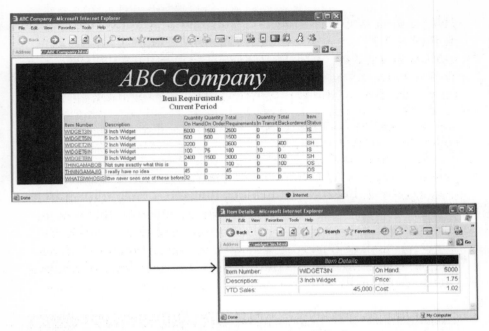

Figure 1.2: The layout of this web application doesn't use JavaScript.

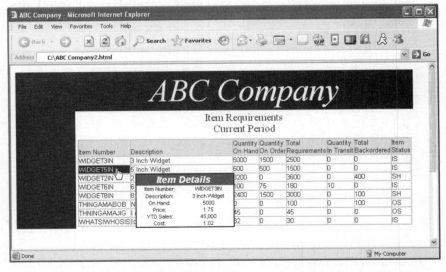

Figure 1.3: This web application is similar to Figure 1.2, but uses JavaScript.

This version of the application displays the same information as in Figure 1.2, but in a small window within the original web page, without having to submit any additional data to the server. This not only helps the application work more efficiently, it also makes the flow of the application smoother for the end-user.

Using a similar technique, it's possible to create a customized right-click context menu for specific items within a page. This context menu could be used to navigate to one of several other pages. Using the ABC Company Item Requirements example from Figure 1.3, you could easily add a context menu to navigate to the item's information screen, place an order for the item, or display warehouse-location information for the item. Each of these options could use the window.open or document.URL operators to either display the information in a new window or navigate to a new URL. An example of this is shown in Figure 1.4.

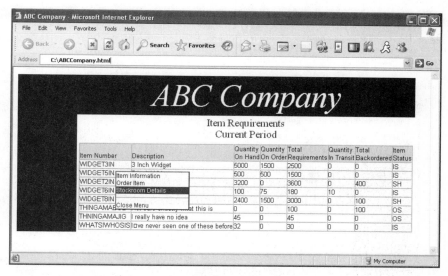

Figure 1.4: The context menu is created using JavaScript.

Again, the addition of this type of user-interface element allows you to make web applications act more like other business applications. Ultimately, this helps your users work more efficiently.

User-Customizable Views

Since different people have different work habits, a single, fixed user interface might not be efficient for all individuals. If you give users the ability to customize elements within a web application, you can help them achieve greater productivity and make their jobs easier. Using JavaScript, you can easily allow users to customize things like color schemes, font styles, and even the location of informational elements within a web application.

For example, consider a sales-reporting dashboard used by sales clerks and sales managers, like the one shown in Figure 1.5. It displays a table of item sales on the bottom of the screen, a chart of sales by region on the top-left side of the screen, and a chart of regional sales by quarter on the top-right of the screen.

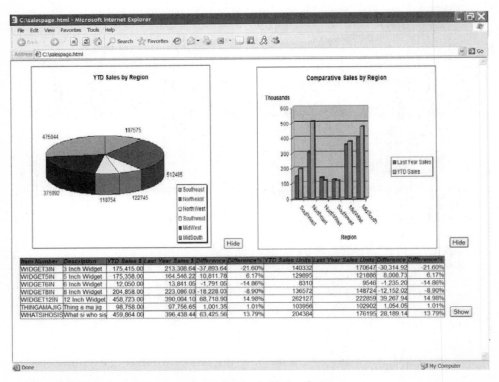

Figure 1.5: Web page elements can be customized with JavaScript.

For a sales clerk, the most important piece of information might be the table of sales by item. She might want to hide the sales charts to make more room for that table, as shown in Figure 1.6.

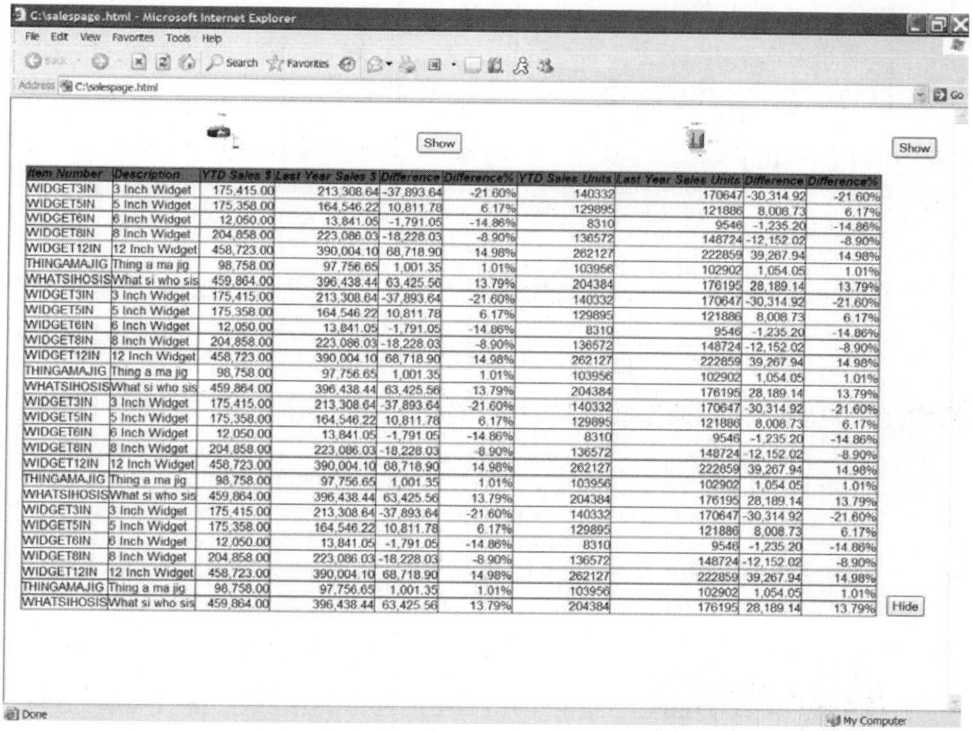

Item Number	Description	YTD Sales $	Last Year Sales $	Difference	Difference%	YTD Sales Units	Last Year Sales Units	Difference	Difference%
WIDGET3IN	3 Inch Widget	175,415.00	213,308.64	-37,893.64	-21.60%	140332	170647	-30,314.92	-21.60%
WIDGET5IN	5 Inch Widget	175,358.00	164,546.22	10,811.78	6.17%	129895	121886	8,008.73	6.17%
WIDGET6IN	6 Inch Widget	12,050.00	13,841.05	-1,791.05	-14.86%	8310	9546	-1,235.20	-14.86%
WIDGET8IN	8 Inch Widget	204,858.00	223,086.03	-18,228.03	-8.90%	136572	148724	-12,152.02	-8.90%
WIDGET12IN	12 Inch Widget	458,723.00	390,004.10	68,718.90	14.98%	262127	222859	39,267.94	14.98%
THINGAMAJIG	Thing a ma jig	98,758.00	97,756.65	1,001.35	1.01%	103956	102902	1,054.05	1.01%
WHATSIHOSIS	What si who sis	459,864.00	396,438.44	63,425.56	13.79%	204384	176195	28,189.14	13.79%
WIDGET3IN	3 Inch Widget	175,415.00	213,308.64	-37,893.64	-21.60%	140332	170647	-30,314.92	-21.60%
WIDGET5IN	5 Inch Widget	175,358.00	164,546.22	10,811.78	6.17%	129895	121886	8,008.73	6.17%
WIDGET6IN	6 Inch Widget	12,050.00	13,841.05	-1,791.05	-14.86%	8310	9546	-1,235.20	-14.86%
WIDGET8IN	8 Inch Widget	204,858.00	223,086.03	-18,228.03	-8.90%	136572	148724	-12,152.02	-8.90%
WIDGET12IN	12 Inch Widget	458,723.00	390,004.10	68,718.90	14.98%	262127	222859	39,267.94	14.98%
THINGAMAJIG	Thing a ma jig	98,758.00	97,756.65	1,001.35	1.01%	103956	102902	1,054.05	1.01%
WHATSIHOSIS	What si who sis	459,864.00	396,438.44	63,425.56	13.79%	204384	176195	28,189.14	13.79%
WIDGET3IN	3 Inch Widget	175,415.00	213,308.64	-37,893.64	-21.60%	140332	170647	-30,314.92	-21.60%
WIDGET5IN	5 Inch Widget	175,358.00	164,546.22	10,811.78	6.17%	129895	121886	8,008.73	6.17%
WIDGET6IN	6 Inch Widget	12,050.00	13,841.05	-1,791.05	-14.86%	8310	9546	-1,235.20	-14.86%
WIDGET8IN	8 Inch Widget	204,858.00	223,086.03	-18,228.03	-8.90%	136572	148724	-12,152.02	-8.90%
WIDGET12IN	12 Inch Widget	458,723.00	390,004.10	68,718.90	14.98%	262127	222859	39,267.94	14.98%
THINGAMAJIG	Thing a ma jig	98,758.00	97,756.65	1,001.35	1.01%	103956	102902	1,054.05	1.01%
WHATSIHOSIS	What si who sis	459,864.00	396,438.44	63,425.56	13.79%	204384	176195	28,189.14	13.79%
WIDGET3IN	3 Inch Widget	175,415.00	213,308.64	-37,893.64	-21.60%	140332	170647	-30,314.92	-21.60%
WIDGET5IN	5 Inch Widget	175,358.00	164,546.22	10,811.78	6.17%	129895	121886	8,008.73	6.17%
WIDGET6IN	6 Inch Widget	12,050.00	13,841.05	-1,791.05	-14.86%	8310	9546	-1,235.20	-14.86%
WIDGET8IN	8 Inch Widget	204,858.00	223,086.03	-18,228.03	-8.90%	136572	148724	-12,152.02	-8.90%
WIDGET12IN	12 Inch Widget	458,723.00	390,004.10	68,718.90	14.98%	262127	222859	39,267.94	14.98%
THINGAMAJIG	Thing a ma jig	98,758.00	97,756.65	1,001.35	1.01%	103956	102902	1,054.05	1.01%
WHATSIHOSIS	What si who sis	459,864.00	396,438.44	63,425.56	13.79%	204384	176195	28,189.14	13.79%

Figure 1.6: The sales clerk can customize the view to suit his or her needs.

The sales manager, on the other hand, might not be as concerned with item details. He might want to hide that screen component, as shown in Figure 1.7.

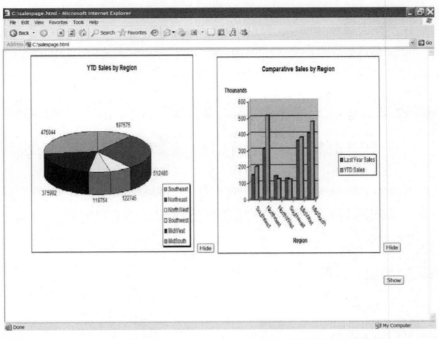

Figure 1.7: A sales manager's view can also be customized to suit his or her individual needs.

With JavaScript, the user can simply click a Hide button to collapse a portion of the document, allowing other parts of the screen to take up the newly available space. Using cookies, the user's preferences can be saved and reapplied each time he or she visits the page. Figure 1.5 through 1.7 illustrate this type of customization.

Allowing users to customize their views of the data adds flexibility and usability to this application. Other customizations might include allowing users to define the color schemes or fonts on their versions of the web application.

Data Manipulation

Along with customizing the look of the screen, it's also possible to manipulate the data shown on the screen using JavaScript. For example, many times an application will display data within a table. Often, users want the flexibility to be able to sort this data by any of the columns in the table. Using JavaScript, it's possible to create a function that sorts the data in a table by a specific column when the user clicks that column. The advantage to using JavaScript for this task is that the sorting is done without having to reload the screen again, improving speed and giving the application a more user-friendly feel.

Figures 1.8 and 1.9 show an example of this type of functionality. Figure 1.8 shows the data sorted by last name.

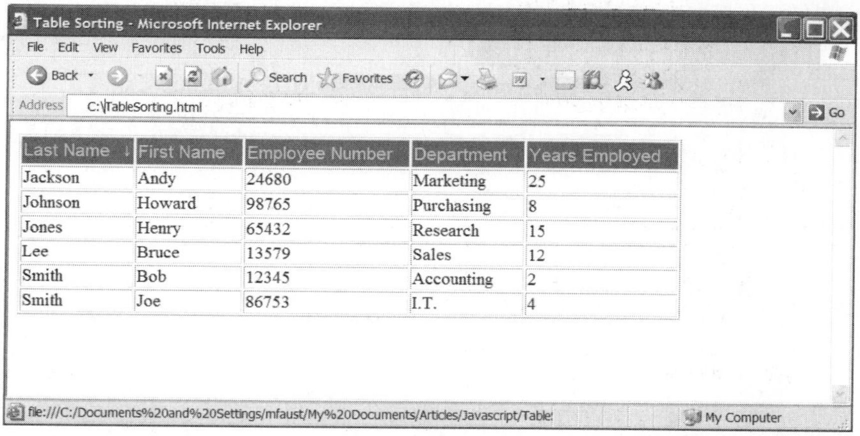

Figure 1.8: JavaScript is used to sort table columns on the fly.

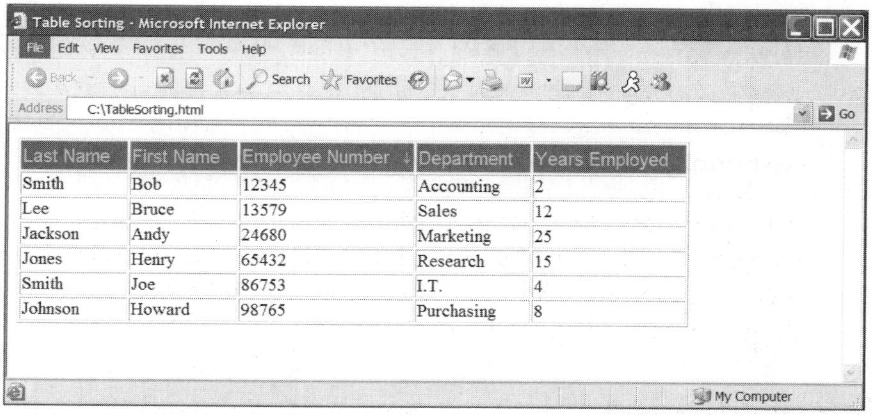

Figure 1.9: A user can change the sort order by clicking on the column headings.

If a user clicks the Employee Number column, the table is instantly re-sorted by that column without having to reload the page, as shown in Figure 1.9. Clicking the column again reverses the sort order from ascending to descending.

Data manipulation can also include performing calculations and displaying the results on the screen, again without submitting the page to the server. For example, you might create a script to recalculate totals as you modify values in a form. The screens in Figures 1.10 and 1.11 illustrate this type of application.

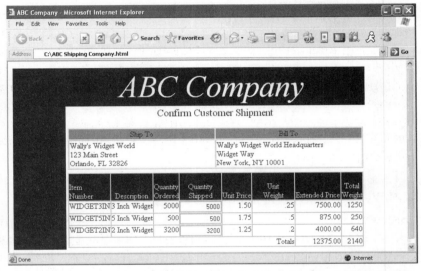

Figure 1.10: Values can be changed in the "Quantity Shipped" column in this web page.

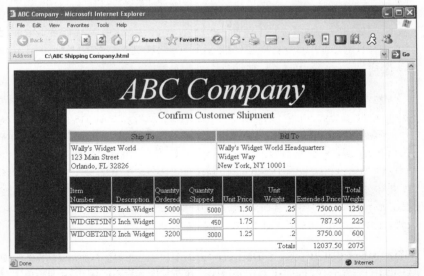

Figure 1.11: The totals displayed are recalculated on the fly in this JavaScript-enabled web page.

In this example, the page is initially presented with values in the text boxes under the "Quantity Shipped" column. A user has the ability to edit these values, which requires the recalculation of any of the other values on the page that are based on the quantity shipped—extended price for example.

As this figure illustrates, once a user changes the value for one of the Shipped Quantity fields, the Total Weight and Extended Line Value columns are recalculated automatically, along with the totals for each of these columns at the bottom of the form. These additional calculated fields can be sent along with the form variables when the form is submitted to the server. In later chapters, you'll learn exactly how to accomplish this type of data manipulation. You'll also see other techniques for changing the contents of a page on the fly.

Integrating with Backend Systems

Since browser-based applications are true client-server applications, it's important to understand how JavaScript can be used to communicate with remote systems. JavaScript can't read data using any of the common database APIs, such as ODBC or JDBC. However, JavaScript can read and display data from an XML data source. With the growing influx of XML web services, your JavaScript-based application has access to a plethora of information providers. Using JavaScript, it's actually possible to access all elements of an XML document.

The application in Figure 1.12 accepts a zip code, consumes two free web services to obtain data, and then returns one week's forecast data from the National Weather Service (NWS). The NWS application requires longitude and latitude values to retrieve weather information. The longitude and latitude values for a given zip code can be determined using a free web service from Yahoo.com's Maps web site. This web service also returns the city and state associated with the zip code.

The information returned from the NWS web service includes links to the graphics associated with the forecast for each day. The data retrieved is used to fill in a predefined HTML table, giving a nice display of the forecast data. By simply changing the entered zip code and pressing the Get Forecast button, JavaScript replaces the current forecast with one for the desired location. This is all done on the client, without ever having to connect to a web server (other than the servers providing the XML data, of course).

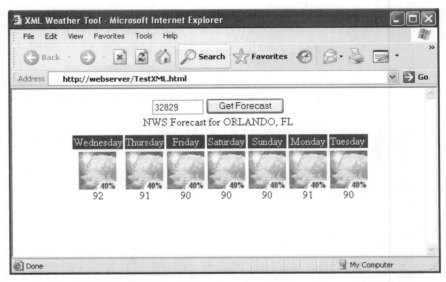

Figure 1.12: This page consumes XML web services to access data.

This example could easily be incorporated into another web page, allowing you to give weather forecast data along with whatever other information is displayed by the application. (In chapter 6, you'll see exactly how this example was created.) While this example uses freely available public web services, you could use the same technique to create JavaScript applications that consume private XML web services built into, say, your ERP system. This helps to illustrate why designing applications with Service Oriented Architecture (SOA) in mind makes so much sense, since web services are the only way to be able to access remote data sources in JavaScript.

Suppose that you need to create an application programming interface (API) to retrieve customer-order data. If you build this API as a web service, you add the ability to use it from many other development platforms (including JavaScript).

Let's assume that the data in Figure 1.13 was generated by an XML web service that interfaces to your ERP application. This data could easily be read and displayed to the browser using client-side JavaScript. Multiple items, such as the order-detail lines in this example, can be accessed within JavaScript as a collection or array.

```xml
<?xml version="1.0" encoding="ISO-8859-1" ?>
- <ORDER>
  - <HEADER>
        <ORDER_NUMBER>0123456</ORDER_NUMBER>
        <CUSTOMER_NUMBER>45678</CUSTOMER_NUMBER>
        <CUSTOMER_NAME>Wally's Widget World</CUSTOMER_NAME>
        <ORDER_DATE>12/15/2006</ORDER_DATE>
        <SHIP_VIA>FEDEX</SHIP_VIA>
    </HEADER>
  - <DETAILS>
    - <LINE>
              <ORDER_LINE>1</ORDER_LINE>
              <ITEM>WIDGET3IN</ITEM>
              <DESCRIPTION>3 Inch Widget</DESCRIPTION>
              <QUANTITY>500</QUANTITY>
              <PRICE>1.25</PRICE>
      </LINE>
    - <LINE>
              <ORDER_LINE>2</ORDER_LINE>
              <ITEM>WIDGET5IN</ITEM>
              <DESCRIPTION>5 Inch Widget</DESCRIPTION>
              <QUANTITY>250</QUANTITY>
              <PRICE>1.55</PRICE>
      </LINE>
    - <LINE>
              <ORDER_LINE>1</ORDER_LINE>
              <ITEM>WIDGET2IN</ITEM>
              <DESCRIPTION>5 Inch Widget</DESCRIPTION>
              <QUANTITY>1000</QUANTITY>
              <PRICE>1.15</PRICE>
      </LINE>
    - <LINE>
              <ORDER_LINE>4</ORDER_LINE>
              <ITEM>WIDGET6IN</ITEM>
              <DESCRIPTION>6 Inch Widget</DESCRIPTION>
              <QUANTITY>1500</QUANTITY>
              <PRICE>1.75</PRICE>
      </LINE>
    </DETAILS>
  </ORDER>
```

Figure 1.13: This example shows XML data returned by an ERP application.

This type of interaction between JavaScript and XML has become more prevalent with the introduction of Asynchronous XML and JavaScript (AJAX). This technology basically encompasses the ability to send and request XML data via JavaScript. You'll see more examples of AJAX in chapter 6.

Server-Side Interaction

While there is no direct link between a server-side technology like ASP or PHP and client-side JavaScript, there are ways for the two technologies to interact. The primary way is through HTML form elements. Items like <input> boxes can be used to pass data values between JavaScript and web server-side scripts. The use of an <input> box with a type of "hidden" allows a script programmer to send an "invisible" variable to the server. It's also possible to pass these values from "hidden" variables back to your page from the server-side script, since server-side scripting languages can create HTML elements on the fly. Figure 1.14 illustrates this technique.

This ability to dynamically create web page elements from a server-side script also includes the ability to conditionally write out JavaScript code from the server side. JavaScript is processed in-line as the page is read in, which means that a script embedded within a cell of an HTML table is processed when that cell is displayed. Dynamically writing out JavaScript code from the server-side language gives you the ability to totally customize the user experience from the server. You might use this technique to conditionally enable or disable elements of the user interface, like the context menus you saw earlier in this chapter.

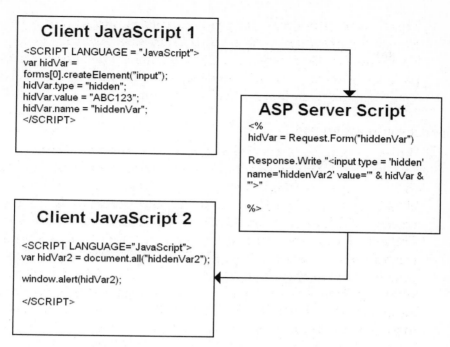

Figure 1.14: Data can be passed between JavaScript and server-side scripts.

Summary

Now that you've seen some of the justifications for business programmers as to *why* to use JavaScript, it's time to start examining *how* to use JavaScript. In chapter 2, you'll learn exactly what JavaScript is.

CHAPTER 2

JavaScript 101

The JavaScript language was developed by a Netscape programmer named Brendan Eich. Originally called "LiveScript," it was introduced with Netscape Navigator version 2.0 in September, 1995. In December of that year, LiveScript was renamed JavaScript because of the scripting language's similarity in structure to Java. In July of 1996, Microsoft introduced their port of JavaScript (called "Jscript") as a component of Internet Explorer 3.0. The Netscape and Microsoft implementations of JavaScript, even today, have significant differences in their object models. (You'll learn about these differences a little later in this chapter.) Today, JavaScript offers a robust client-side language for creating dynamic and vibrant browser-based applications.

What Is JavaScript?

Before going any further, let's explore exactly what JavaScript is (and is *not*). While the syntax used within JavaScript is similar to the Java programming language, JavaScript is not Java, nor is it a subset of Java. There is a common misconception that JavaScript is somehow related to the Java programming language. This is absolutely false. Java is a full-featured, complex programming language. JavaScript, in contrast, is an interpreted scripting language. This means that no compilation occurs prior to the execution of JavaScript code.

JavaScript allows a programmer to control and enhance the user interface offered by applications running within popular web browsers. JavaScript code is generally embedded within an HTML web page or similar document (such as an XML document). Alternatively, it can be contained within its own source file and then referenced in HTML and XML documents. It's important to note that there is also a "server-side" JavaScript component, which is supported by Netscape's Enterprise Server product. This product allows the use of JavaScript as a server-scripting language. All discussions of JavaScript as a language in this book refer to the client-side scripting language.

Blocks of JavaScript code are contained in HTML documents within the <script> tag. For example, in the following code segment, the JavaScript document.write() statement is executed:

```
<SCRIPT LANGUAGE = "JavaScript">
document.write("JavaScript Code");
</SCRIPT>
```

Note the "language" parameter of the <script> tag, which describes the specific scripting language to be used to interpret the script.

If the JavaScript code is in its own file, you include that file in your HTML document, as shown here:

```
<SCRIPT LANGUAGE = "JavaScript" SRC = "myjavascript.js">
```

When the page containing this <script> block is loaded, the file "myjavascript.js" will be loaded as well, and the JavaScript source in that file will be executed. This technique can be very convenient for commonly used JavaScript functions.

One very important note about JavaScript as a language is that it is interpreted by the browser. Therefore, it's possible that different browsers may react to the same JavaScript source code differently. In fact, two distinctly different versions of JavaScript currently exist. This needs to be taken into consideration when writing JavaScript source that may be executed within different browser platforms. To make this a bit easier, let's take a look at the different "flavors" of JavaScript.

A Script by Any Other Name

As you've already discovered, the original version of JavaScript was developed by Netscape. Microsoft (as it so often does) has also developed its own "flavor" of JavaScript, known as JScript. Netscape's version of JavaScript is generally supported on any Mozilla-based browser (such as Netscape Navigator or Firefox), while JScript is supported primarily on Microsoft's Internet Explorer.

To help reconcile the differences in JavaScript implementations, Microsoft and Netscape agreed to a vendor-neutral standard defined by the European Computer Manufacturer's Association. *ECMAScript*, as this standard is known, was originally agreed upon in 1997. The complete ECMAScript standard can be found on the ECMA web site at *http://www.ecma-international.org*.

Even with this standard in place, there are still significant differences in the two scripting languages. Although JavaScript and JScript can interact with their prospective web browsers in significantly different ways, it is possible to code your script to deal with these differences. Because of the ECMAScript standard, the primary differences are found, not so much in the language structure itself, but in the document object model supported by the browser platform under which each language runs.

DOM Implementations Compared

The *document object model (DOM)* is a hierarchical structure used to access all of the objects within an HTML document. The World Wide Web Consortium (W3C) has a defined DOM standard. The current version, referred to as *Level 3*, was defined in 2004. Each browser's level of compliance with the W3C standard varies. The general "tree" structure shown in Figure 2.1 is common to all implementations, however.

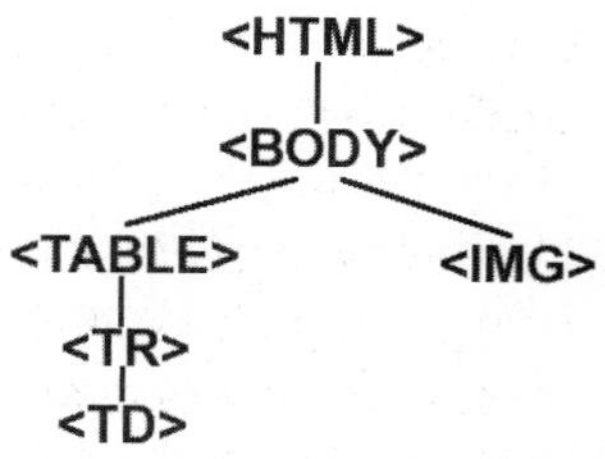

```
        <HTML>
          |
        <BODY>
        /      \
  <TABLE>      <IMG>
     |
   <TR>
     |
   <TD>
```

Figure 2.1: An illustration of DOM's tree structure.

The variety of browsers and versions of browsers makes it difficult to come up with a comprehensive list of differences in compatibility. Rather than try to explain all of these differences, let's focus on how to identify and deal with the differences when they occur.

Test...Test...Test

Probably the most important rule when developing JavaScript applications that are compliant with multiple browsers is to test your code on multiple browsers. While this might seem obvious, it can be easy to get into the habit of writing script code that is primarily tested on your "browser of choice." Later, you find out that some portion of the code is incompatible with another browser. On a side note, this is not always a bad thing. If you're designing applications to be used in a "controlled environment" such as your office, you might not care that the code is compatible with a browser your IT staff does not wish to support.

That said, it's a good idea to have access to as many different browsers as possible to test your JavaScript code on. Most problems will present themselves immediately. To illustrate this, look at the following HTML document:

```
<html>
<body>
My Test Page
</body>
<script type="text/javascript">
Window.navigate("http://www.w3.org");
</Script>
</html>
```

When this page is loaded in Internet Explorer, it immediately redirects to the *w3.org* web page. When the page is loaded in a Netscape browser, however, the document doesn't redirect because the window.navigate() statement is not supported by Netscape's JavaScript implementation. To allow this page to be compatible with both browsers, the statement should be replaced with the following line of code, which is accepted by both:

```
window.location.href = "http://www.w3.org";
```

Test your script within as many browser environments as possible to ensure complete browser compatibility before deployment, rather than discovering after the fact that your script code is not browser independent. A good rule of thumb is to use "browser neutral" code whenever possible. In some circumstances, however, this will not be possible. In those cases, it is possible to code your scripts to be "browser aware" and, as a result, execute code specific to each individual browser only when the page is being displayed on that browser.

Determining Browser Environments

When your scripts will be run in an "uncontrolled" environment, where you can't mandate which specific browser will be used, it's important that your code can determine what browser it's running on. Fortunately, there is a way to have your JavaScript code do exactly that. The key to this ability is JavaScript's "navigator" object. Note that the word navigator is all in lowercase—it's important to remember that the JavaScript language is case-sensitive.

The "navigator" object gives you the ability to determine many different pieces of information related to the browser environment in which the page is being displayed. Table 2.1 lists the methods and properties supported by this object. As you can see, it allows you to retrieve pertinent information related to both the client browser and operating system. Using this information, it's easy to determine what browser is displaying the object.

Table 2.1: The Properties and Methods of the "navigator" Object	
Method	**Description**
appCodeName	This value identifies the code name associated with the browser (Mozilla, for example).
appMinorVersion	This is the minor version number associated with the browser (SP2, for example).
AppName	This value identifies the full name of the browser product, such as Microsoft Internet Explorer.
cookieEnabled	This returns a "true/false" value indicating whether or not the cookies are enabled on the browser for storing data.
cpuClass	This value identifies the type of CPU on the client computer (x86, for example).
mimeTypes	This contains an array of the MIME types supported by the browser.
onLine	This returns a "true/false" value indicating whether or not the client computer is connected to the Internet.
platform	This property returns a value representing the client platform on which the page is being displayed (Win32, for example).
plugins	This method returns an array of values indicating any plug-in installed on and supported by the browser.
systemLanguage	This property returns a value indicating the default operating system language on the system displaying the document.
userAgent	This returns the HTML user-agent string, such as Mozilla/4.0 (compatible; MSIE 6.0; Windows NT 5.1).
userLanguage	This property returns the natural language setting for the operating system of the system displaying the document.

Figure 2.2 is an example of a script that supports specific code for different browsers. This script begins by defining a variable to contain the value of the navigator.userAgent property as a lower-case string. This value is then compared to several possible values, using "if" statements. If the condition of a statement evaluates to true, the code required for that specific browser is executed. This simple, yet effective, method can be used whenever browser-specific code is needed.

```
<script type="text/javascript">
var usrAgt=navigator.userAgent.toLowerCase();
if (usrAgt.indexOf("firefox") != -1) {
// Firefox specific code goes here
}
if (usrAgt.indexOf("msie") != -1) {
// Internet Explorer specific code goes here
}
if (usrAgt.indexOf("netscape") != -1) {
// Netscape specific code goes here
}
if (usrAgt.indexOf("opera") != -1) {
// Opera specific code goes here
}
if (usrAgt.indexOf("mozilla/5.0") != -1) {
// Mozilla specific code goes here
}
</script>
```

Figure 2.2: This script illustrates how to determine the browser.

JavaScript/HTML Interaction

Because the main purpose of the JavaScript language is to control components of an HTML-based web page, it's important to understand exactly how JavaScript and HTML interact. JavaScript source can exist in one of two methods: an internally defined script embedded directly in the HTML document, or an external script defined within its own file. In both cases, the <script> HTML tag is the key to defining your script.

To embed JavaScript source within a web page, you define the <script> tag as shown here:

```
<script type="text/javascript">
var usrAgt = navigator.userAgent;
window.alert(usrAgt);
</script>
```

In an embedded script, the actual JavaScript source is simply placed between the opening and closing <script> tags. In some cases, however, you might have code that will be used in multiple web pages. Rather than placing the same code in each HTML document, it's possible to save this code within its own file and incorporate that script file in your HTML document. Here is an example of the HTML source to do this:

```
<script src="myscript.js" type="text/javascript">
</script>
```

In this example, the "src" attribute defines the location of the file containing the JavaScript source. This file should be saved with a ".js" extension.

The location of the <script> tag within your HTML document can affect the way your script executes, so there are a few general rules to keep in mind. First, any JavaScript functions to be called from within the HTML document should be placed in the <head> section of the document, as shown here:

```
<html>
<head>
<script src="functions.js" type="text/javascript">
</script>
</head>
<body>
</body>
</html>
```

This example uses an external JavaScript file named "functions.js." Placing JavaScript functions within the <head> section ensures that these functions will be available as soon as the page loads. If this script was placed at the end of the document, any problem with loading it could prevent the JavaScript functions from being accessible.

On the other hand, JavaScript source that is intended to be executed as part of the page load should be placed within the <body> section of the document. The document below illustrates the use of an embedded script this way:

```
<html>
<head>
<script src="functions.js" type="text/javascript">
</script>
</head>
<body>
<h1 align=center>My Web Page</h1><br>
<script type="text/javascript">
var usrAgt = navigator.userAgent;
document.write("<h3 align=center>" + usrAgt + "</h3>");
</script>
<h2 align=center>Bottom</h2>
</body>
</html>
```

This example uses navigator.userAgent and displays the resulting value of userAgent to the browser, as shown in Figure 2.3.

It's important to remember that the script will be executed wherever it is placed. Therefore, if there were objects before the JavaScript, they would be displayed before the output from the script would be generated. Similarly, any objects after this script would be displayed after the output from the JavaScript code.

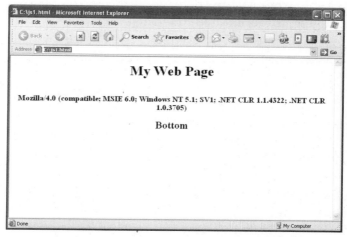

Figure 2.3: This output is generated by a JavaScript function.

As you can see from Figure 2.3, the portion of the page created using JavaScript is placed exactly where the JavaScript source is located. This example helps to illustrate the way that JavaScript and HTML are intertwined. When creating truly interactive web applications, they are both important components.

It's also important to understand how HTML objects are accessed and manipulated within JavaScript. In Figure 2.1, you saw the hierarchical tree structure that makes up an HTML web page. Any of the objects within the tree structure can be accessed from within JavaScript. One of the easiest ways to do this is to assign an ID attribute on the <html> tag for the object. (Within this discussion, an object is considered an HTML tag and any elements found before the matching ending HTML tag. For example, an HTML <table> contains all of the objects defined before the closing </table> tag.)

The example below defines an ID attribute for an HTML table:

```
<table id="MyTable">
<tr><td>Cell 1</td></tr>
<tr><td>Cell 2</td></tr>
<tr><td>Cell 3</td></tr>
</table>
```

In this example, the HTML table is named "MyTable." To access this table from within the page's JavaScript, you need to use the getElementById method, like this:

```
<script type="text/javascript">
var vrTable = document.getElementById("MyTable");
</script>
```

This example creates a variable that contains the HTML table object. This variable will inherit all of the properties and methods of the object. So, once this variable has been defined, all of the rows and cells within the HTML table can be accessed using this new object. You can even add and remove rows and columns from the table.

In addition to using document.getElementById(), you can access objects within an HTML document in several other ways. The document.documentElements object, for example, gives you access to the <html> tag itself. Similarly, the document.body object allows access to the <body> tag directly. This tag is a child of the <html> tag, and could also be accessed through the childNodes collection. In fact, this collection can be used to read through the entire hierarchy of your web page.

The following example uses the childNodes collection to read through all of the first-level objects within an HTML page:

```
<script type="text/javascript">
var bodyTag = document.body;
var children = bodyTag.childNodes.length - 1;

for (var x = 0; x < children; x++) {
    window.alert(bodyTag.childNodes[x].nodeName);
}
</script>
```

This script assigns the variable "bodyTag" to the document.body object. This object is then used to populate the variable "children" with a value equal to the number of child nodes under the <body> tag. This value is used as the upper limit of a "for" loop, to display a message box with the nodeName value for each child node under the <body> tag. Once you've gained access to each child node, you can access the unique properties related to it. For example, you can access each of the rows and cells of a <table> element.

The document.getElementsByTagName() function also allows access to objects within an HTML document. This function returns a collection of elements whose tag matches the value specified on the function's parameter, as shown in Figure 2.4.

```html
<html>
    <head></head>
    <body>
        <table id = "MyTable">
                <tr><td>Cell1</td><td>Cell2</td></tr>
                <tr><td>Cell3</td><td>Cell4</td></tr>
        </table>

        <table id = "MyTable2">
                <tr><td>Cell5</td><td>Cell6</td></tr>
                <tr><td>Cell7</td><td>Cell8</td></tr>
        </table>
    </body>

    <script type="text/javascript">
        var tbls = document.getElementsByTagName("table");
        var kids = tbls.length;

        for (var x = 0; x < kids; x++) {
            var y = (x + 1).toString();
            document.write("Table " + y + " = " + tbls[x].id + "<br>");
        }
    </script>
</html>
```

Figure 2.4: This HTML page illustrates the use of getElementsByTagName().

This example contains two tables that each contain two rows, and two cells per row. The JavaScript code uses getElementsByTagName() to search for all table elements within the document. The script then runs through the returned collection and displays a line at the bottom of the page indicating the ID value for each table.

This example also illustrates how JavaScript can be used to dynamically add information to a page after it has been loaded into your browser. In this example, the original page only contained two tables, with four cells each. After the JavaScript is executed, two lines of text containing information about the tables are added to the page, as shown in Figure 2.5. This type of dynamic change can be used in much more interesting (and flashy) ways, as you'll see a little later on in this book.

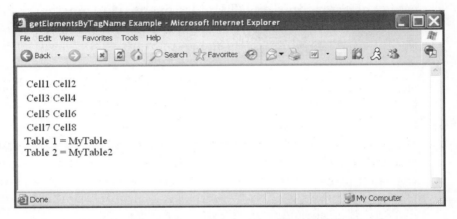

Figure 2.5: The last two lines were generated using getElementsByTagName().

JavaScript also supports several element-specific objects to access individual objects within your HTML document. A good example of this is the forms collection, which is accessed through document.forms(). This collection allows access to all of the HTML form objects in your web page. It is basically a shortcut to using the statement document.getElementsByTagName("form"). You can then access any of the objects within the form using the "elements" collection. Figure 2.6 contains a sample of using both the "forms" and "elements" collections.

```
<html>
    <head>
        <title>"forms" and "elements" collections</title>
    </head>
    <body>
        <form name = "MyForm">
            <input type="Text" name="field1">
            <input type="Button" value = "submit" name="btn1">
        </form>
    </body>

    <script type="text/javascript">
        var myForm = document.forms["MyForm"];
        var fields = myForm.length;

        for (var x = 0; x < fields; x++) {
            var y = (x + 1).toString();
            document.write(myForm.elements[x].name + " = " +
              myForm.elements[x].type  + "<br>");
        }
    </script>
</html>
```

Figure 2.6: The "forms" and "elements" collections are used to read form data.

When executed, this script accesses the form "MyForm" via the "forms" collection. It then uses the "elements" collection to read each object within the form and display the object's name and type to the browser window. Figure 2.7 shows the output generated by this code.

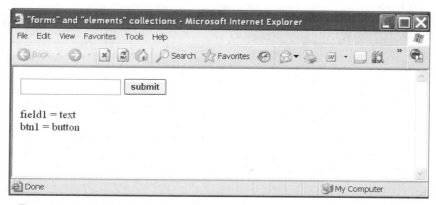

Figure 2.7: JavaScript is used here to read HTML form data.

Accessing form fields this way enables you to pre-edit the fields, to ensure that values have been supplied for required fields before submitting the form. Where the fields' valid values are based on easily verifiable values like date ranges, you can extend this technique to do validity-checking.

Table 2.2 lists the collections of the document object that allow direct access to specific web page elements. Each of these collections allows JavaScript to access each of the corresponding HTML tags within the document. As with the earlier examples, each of these collections is based on the "document" object, which gives access to the top level of the HTML document.

Table 2.2: Using JavaScript to Read HTML Form Data		
Collection	**Related Tag**	**Description**
Anchors	<a>	This collection gives access to all hyperlinks within the HTML document.
Applets	<applet>	This collection gives access to Java applets within the HTML document.
Forms	<form>	This collection gives access to all forms within the HTML document.
Images	<img>	This collection gives access to all image elements within the HTML document.

Other details about the HTML page can be retrieved through the "document" object, as well. Document.domain retrieves the domain name of the document being displayed (*www.mcpressonline.com*, for example). Document.referrer lets you determine the page that preceded the current page via link or form submission. Document.title retrieves the value of the <title> HTML tag, which defines the text to be displayed in the web browser's title bar. This property can also be updated from within JavaScript, so you can change the title bar text dynamically, as shown in this example:

```
<html>
        <head>
                <title>My Page</title>
        </head>

        <script type="text/javascript">
                var ttl = document.title;
                var curDate = new Date();

                document.title = ttl + " " + curDate;
        </script>
</html>
```

This code loads the document title "My Page" into the variable ttl. Next, the variable curDate is populated with the current date and time. Then, the document.title property is changed by appending the current date to the end of the original title. Figure 2.8 shows the output from this example.

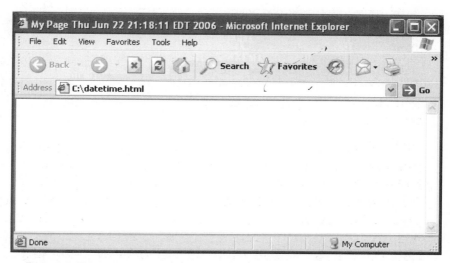

Figure 2.8: This example updates the title bar dynamically.

Finally, document.URL retrieves the fully qualified uniform resource locator (URL) address for the document (such as *http://www.mc-store.com/mikefaust.html*). The URL property is also updatable, allowing you to redirect to another page or web site if a specified page has a problem or is under construction, as shown in this example:

```
<script type="text/javascript">
        var pgURL = document.URL;

        if (pgURL = "brokenpage.html") {
        document.URL = "redirectedpage.html";
        }
</script>
```

While each these properties might not be very useful in a script that was embedded in a single web page, remember that JavaScript source can be stored in an external (.js) file and used in multiple web pages. These external JavaScript files can be written to perform specific tasks based on the values of these properties, or to update the updatable properties. For example, an external JavaScript might be set to dynamically set the title property with the date and time, as in Figure 2.8. This external JavaScript might then be included in all of the pages of a web site for consistency purposes.

Summary

Hopefully, this chapter has given you a good idea of what JavaScript is and how it works within a web page. In the coming chapters, you'll explore the JavaScript language structure itself and how to make the most of it to create dynamic business applications.

3

JavaScript Language Elements

The first two chapters focused on the conceptual aspects of JavaScript for business programmers. Now it's time to examine the nuts and bolts of the JavaScript language itself.

Language Structure and Syntax

As you learned in the previous chapters, JavaScript shares many of its syntax and language elements with other languages like Java. Lines of JavaScript code, for example, must end with a semicolon (;) character. Therefore, in the sample code below, the first statement is coded correctly, while the second statement is not:

```
x = 12;

y = x + 5
```

Groups of JavaScript statements that define functions, "for" loops, and conditional statements (such as "if" and "while") must be surrounded by the curly bracket characters { and }. The following statements show the use of curly brackets with an "if" statement nested inside of a function:

```
Function myFunc(x) {
  if (x > 12) {
    x = 1;
    y = x + 1;
  }
}
```

JavaScript supports a variety of operators for performing string and numeric operations. Table 3.1 lists these operators, along with descriptions of their uses. Many of these operators share their format with those in Java and C++.

Table 3.1: JavaScript Operators		
Operator	**Type**	**Description**
+	Numeric	Addition (result = value1 + value2)
-	Numeric	Subtraction (result = value1 - value2)
*	Numeric	Multiplication (result = value1 * value2)
/	Numeric	Division (result = value1 / value2)
%	Numeric	Modulus—remainder after division(result = value1 % value2)
++	Numeric (Unary)	Increment by 1 (result++)
—	Numeric (Unary)	Decrement by 1 (result—)
+	String	Concatenate (stringreslut = string1 + string2)
==	Comparison	Equal to (value1 == value2)
!=	Comparison	Not equal to (value1 != value2)
>	Comparison	Greater than (value1 > value2)
>=	Comparison	Greater than or equal to (value1 >= value2)
<	Comparison	Less than (value1 < value2)
<=	Comparison	Less than or equal to (value1 <= value2)
===	Comparison	Identical—equal to with type comparison (value1 === value2)
!==	Comparison	Not identical (value1 !== value2)
=	Assignment	Set value (result = value)
+=	Assignment	Increment and set (result += 12 would be the same as result = result + 12)
-=	Assignment	Decrement and set (result -= 12)
*=	Assignment	Multiply and set (result *= 2)
/=	Assignment	Divide and set (result /= 3)
%=	Assignment	Modulus and set (result %= 6)
&=	Assignment	Bitwise AND and set value (result &= value)
|=	Assignment	Bitwise OR and set value (result |= value)
^=	Assignment	Bitwise XOR and set value (result |= value)

Operator	Type	Description
<<=	Assignment	Bitwise left-shift with zero-fill, and set value (result <<= 2)
>>=	Assignment	Bitwise right-shift, self-propagating, and set value (result >>= 2)
>>>=	Assignment	Bitwise right-shift with zero-fill, and set value (result >>>= 2)
&&	Boolean	Logical AND if(val1=1 && val2=2)
||	Boolean	Logical OR if(val1=1 || val2=2)
!	Boolean	Logical NOT (if !(val1 = val2))
&	Bitwise	Bitwise AND (result = val1 & val2
|	Bitwise	Bitwise OR (result = val1 & val2)
~	Bitwise	Bitwise NOT (result =!bit1)
<<	Bitwise	Bitwise left-shift with zero-fill (result = 8 << 2)
>>	Bitwise	Bitwise right-shift, self-propagating (result = 8 >> 2)
>>>	Bitwise	Bitwise right-shift with zero-fill (result = 8 >>> 2)

Table 3.1: JavaScript Operators

The simple numeric operators for performing addition, subtraction, multiplication, and division are fairly self-explanatory. The modulus operator performs a division of two values or variables and returns the remainder as the result. For example, the following line of code would return a value of four, since 18 divided by seven is two, with a remainder of four:

```
result = 18 % 7;
```

Most of the comparison operators are fairly self-explanatory as well, with the exception of the identical (===) and not identical (!==) operators. Each of these operators performs a comparison of two supplied variables based not only on their values, but on their types as well. The following code illustrates this:

```
var x1 = 12;
var x2 = "12";

if (x1 == x2) {
document.write("Equal! ");
}
if (x1 !== x2) {
document.write("But NOT Identical!");
```

In this example, *x1* is defined as a numeric variable with a value of 12, and *x2* is a string variable with a value of "12." A comparison of these two using the "==" operator evaluates to true. With the "===" operator, however, the condition evaluates to false because one variable is a string, while the other is numeric.

Assignment operators are used to set or modify the value of a variable. The "=" operator simply sets the value of a variable based on another value or formula. Several extensions to this operator allow you to perform a calculation based on the variable being assigned the value. For example, the two statements below will return the same result:

```
x1 = x1 + 24;

x1 += 24;
```

Both of these statements increment the value of the variable x1 by 24. The "+=" operator increments the variable used with the operator by the value following the operator. Similarly, the "-=" operator decreases the supplied variable by the value supplied to the right of the operator, and the "*=" and "/=" operators multiply or divide the supplied variable by that value.

The "%=" operator can be used to perform a modulus operation on the result variable using the value supplied on the right side of the operator. The two statements below illustrate two methods of performing this operation:

```
remNdr1 = remNdr1 % 7;

remNdr1 %= 7;
```

In both of these examples, the value of remNdr1 is divided by seven. The remainder from this division operation is then assigned to the remNdr1 variable.

Boolean operators are used to compare multiple conditions within an expression such as an "if" statement. Following are examples of "if" statements using each of these operators:

```
' Boolean AND condition
if (x > 1 && x < 12) {
}

' Boolean OR condition
if (x < 1 || x > 12) {
}

' Boolean NOT condition
if (!(x =6)) {
}
```

Bitwise operators allow you to perform operations on a variable at a bit level and, in the case of bitwise assignment operators, re-assign the result to that same variable. The bitwise AND (&), OR (|), and NOT (!) operators function similarly to the Boolean operators. In addition to these operators, there are also operators that let you shift data bits to the right or left by a specified number of bits. These operators include "&=" for bitwise AND operations, "|=" for bitwise OR, "^=" for bitwise XOR (exclusive OR), "<<=" to shift bits to the left and shift in zeros from the right, ">>=" to shift bits to the right, and finally ">>>=" to shift bits to the right and shift in zeros from the left. Table 3.2 illustrates the functionality performed by some of the bitwise operators.

Table 3.2: JavaScript Bitwise Operators	
Statement	**Operation Description**
X = 7 & 43;	00000111 & 00101011 = 00000011 = 3
X= 7	43	00000111	00101011 = 00101111 = 47
X= ^7	~ 0111 = -1000 = -8
<<	0000 0100 << 4 = 0100 0000 or 4 << 4 = 64
>>	0000 1100 >> 2 = 0000 0011 or 12 >> 2 = 3
>>>	0000 1100 >>> 2 = 0000 0011 or 12 >>> 2 = 3

The primary difference between the two right-shift operators is that the ">>>" operator moves zeros in from the left after the shift is performed, while ">>" moves in the leftmost bit. Because of this, positive numbers will appear the same, while negative numbers will appear drastically different.

Declaring Variables and Objects

JavaScript requires the explicit declaration of all variables and objects. The good news is that primitive variables are simple to define. Here is an example of a statement that defines a variable:

```
var myVar
```

This example defines the variable myVar without assigning a value to it. It's also possible to assign an initial value to a variable at the time of declaration, as shown here:

```
var myIntVar = 7;
```

This example declares and initializes the variable in a single statement.

JavaScript language structure is not heavily typed. In fact, only four basic variable types are supported in JavaScript:

- The numeric type for all numeric data
- The string type to hold alphanumeric string data
- The logical (Boolean) type to store "true/false" data
- The null type to store null values

Type declaration is not required when defining JavaScript variables. In fact, a JavaScript variable's type can be redefined without re-declaring the variable, simply by defining a different value, as shown here:

```
<script type="text/javascript">
var myVar = 9;
document.write("myVar + myVar = " + (myVar + myVar) + "<br>");
myVar = "String Text!"
document.write("myVar + myVar = " + (myVar + myVar) + "<br>");
</script>
```

This example declares a variable myVar with an initial value of nine. The document.write() statement is then used to write out the value of this variable, added to itself. Next, the variable is redefined as the string value "String Text!" The value of the variable is again written to the browser, added to itself. Since the "+" operator acts differently for numeric and string variables, the resulting output responds differently in each of these cases. Figure 3.1 shows what the output from this script looks like.

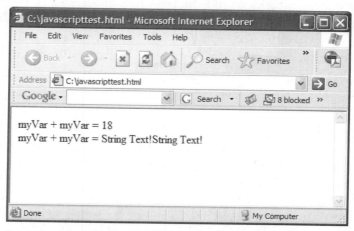

Figure 3.1: Redefining the value of a variable automatically changes its type.

In addition to these simple variable types, JavaScript also supports some more advanced data types, including the array type, the date type, and the object type. As with simple variable declarations, arrays can be both declared and initialized in a single statement by enclosing each of the array element values in square brackets, as shown here:

```
var myArray = ["Sun","Mon","Tue","Wed","Thr","Fri","Sat"];

document.write(myArray[1]);
```

Because JavaScript types are "assumed," the language will identify this variable as an array with seven elements. JavaScript arrays are zero-based, meaning that the first element is 0, the second is 1, and so on. As a result, this example would display the value *Mon*.

It's also possible to explicitly declare a JavaScript array, as shown here:

```
var myArr = Array("A","B","C","D","E","F","G");
```

Note that in this example the square brackets have been replaced by parentheses. It's also important to note that JavaScript only uses memory to store variable elements that actually contain a value. For example, consider this array declaration:

```
var myArr = new Array(12,24,,48,,96);
```

It defines an array with six elements; however, the third and fifth elements contain no values. Unlike other programming languages, JavaScript does not allocate memory space to these array elements. This fact can be valuable when your application needs to define an array for which you may have a large number of elements, but whose elements will be added gradually. This would be defined as shown here for an array of 999 possible elements:

```
var myArr = new Array(999);
```

It's also possible to define multidimensional arrays. This is done by specifying separate "new Array" declarations for each dimension in the array. The example below illustrates this concept:

```
var myArr = new Array(3);
    for (var i=0; i < 3; i++)
    {
        myArr[i] = new Array(3);
        for (var j=0; j < 3; j++)
        {
            myArr[i][j] = "";
        }
    }
```

This example declares a two-dimensional array, where each dimension contains three elements, resulting in nine total elements. This example initializes each element to a blank string. Although the array here is defined with a specific length, an array in JavaScript can be extended by simply defining a new element. For example, the following statement is perfectly acceptable in JavaScript:

```
var myArr = new Array(3);

myArr[9] = "New Element";
```

In this case, the array is initially defined with three elements. By then defining element 9, its length is extended to 10 elements. (Remember, JavaScript arrays are zero-based.) If, on the other hand, you were to refer to an element that had not previously been defined, a value of "undefined" would be returned.

It's also perfectly acceptable to store values of differing types in a JavaScript array. For example, the simple array of three elements defined here is valid:

```
var myArr = new Array("Value 1", 17, 0xFF);
```

JavaScript doesn't care that the first element is a string value, the second is an integer numeric value, and the third element is a hexadecimal value. It's important to note here that JavaScript supports the use of the *0x* prefix to refer to a hexadecimal value. The value is converted to an integer when it is stored in a variable.

JavaScript also supports the definition of user-defined objects through the use of functions. You can create new objects using JavaScript functions because a function can be extended using custom properties and methods that you create on the fly. Figure 3.2 illustrates the creation and use of a simple object.

```
<SCRIPT LANGUAGE=JavaScript>
   var myCircle = new circleBuilder();

   if (myCircle.diameter > 0) {
   myCircle.display();
   }
```

Figure 3.2: JavaScript supports the creation of user-defined objects (part 1 of 2).

```
function circleBuilder() {
    this.radius = prompt("Please Enter the Circle's Radius");
    this.diameter = this.radius * 2;
    this.circumference = Math.PI * this.diameter;
    this.area = Math.PI * this.radius * this.radius;
    this.display = displayCircleInfo;
}

function displayCircleInfo() {
    document.write("A circle with a radius of " + this.radius);
    document.write(" has a diameter of " + this.diameter);
    document.write(", a curcumference of " + this.circumference);
    document.write(" and an area of " + this.area + "<br>");
}
</SCRIPT>
```

Figure 3.2: JavaScript supports the creation of user-defined objects (part 2 of 2).

This example creates an object type named circleBuilder(), which can be used to obtain information about a circle of a given radius. You first create a new object named myCircle, with a defined type of circleBuilder(). When this object is created, the circleBuilder() function prompts the user to enter the desired radius for the circle. Note that the circleBuilder() function is able to reference itself through the use of the "this" object.

The function then calculates various attributes for the circle object and stores those values in individual properties associated with the object. This means that you can access the area of the circle by referencing myCircle.area. You can also create custom methods to perform actions using your user-defined function. The code in Figure 3.2 does this by associating the this.display object with another user-defined function named displayCircleInfo(). If you call the myCircle.display method, the displayCircleInfo() function is called with a reference to the myCircle object. Figures 3.3 and 3.4 show a sample using the circleBuilder() object.

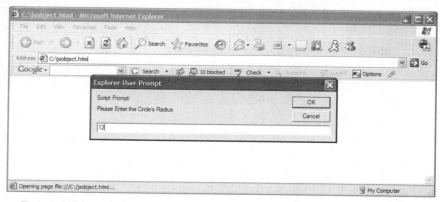

Figure 3.3 This example prompts a user to enter the radius of a circle.

When the page in Figure 3.3 loads, the user is immediately prompted to enter the radius of the circle. This value is passed into the circleBuilder() object. Figure 3.4 shows the results.

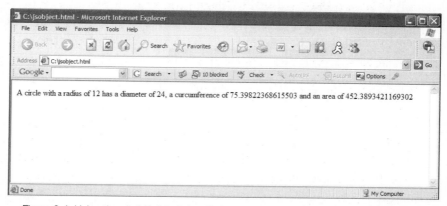

Figure 3.4: Using the circleBuilder() JavaScript object, you can calculate various attributes of a circle.

While this is a relatively simple example, it helps to illustrate how easy it is to use and create custom objects within JavaScript. In this case, the object has both custom properties and custom methods. You'll learn how to create more advanced JavaScript objects a little later.

Flow Control

The JavaScript language has many ways to control application flow. The simplest way is represented by what is called a *conditional operator*. This type of operator conditionally sets a value based on a defined condition, as shown here:

```
x =(y == 0 ? : z: z/y )
```

In this example, if *y* is equal to zero, the value of *x* is set to *z*; otherwise, *x* is set to the value of *z* divided by *y*. This example can be used to avoid potential "divide by zero" errors.

JavaScript also has several statements that let you control the flow of an application based on defined conditions or occurrences. The most basic of these statements is the "if" statement. In JavaScript, the "if" statement uses the following syntax:

```
if (condition) {
    statements to be performed if condition is true
}
else {
statements to be performed if condition is false
}
```

If the defined condition evaluates to true, the program will execute the statements enclosed in the set of curly brackets immediately after the condition.

An "if" can optionally be followed by an "else" that identifies a statement or statements to be executed if the condition does not evaluate to true. The example above uses curly brackets to define a set of statements to be executed. Optionally, a single statement can follow the condition without the use of curly brackets, as shown here:

```
if (x != 1) window.alert("x is not 1");
else window.alert("x is 1");
```

In this example, if *x* is not equal to one, a message is displayed indicating that. The "else" statement is used here to display a message when *x* does equal one.

When you need to conditionally execute different pieces of code based on multiple conditions, use the "else" statement with another "if" statement, as shown below:

```
if (x == 1) {
        x++;
        document.write("this time x was 1");
}
else if (x == 2) {
        x-;
        document.write("this time x was 2");
}
else document.write("x was neither 1 nor 2");
```

This example includes two "if" statements, each testing for different conditions and performing different code segments if their respective conditions are true. Since the second "if" is associated with the "else" statement for the first "if," the second condition will only be checked if the first condition is false. If neither of these conditions are true, the program will execute the code associated with the final "else" statement.

The "switch" and "case" statements are used to perform blocks of code based on several possible values for a single field. These work much like a "select case" statement in other languages. In the example below, each "case" statement compares the value of the variable "animal":

```
switch (animal) {
        case "COW":
                document.write("The Cow Says MOOOOOOOOOOO");
                break;
        case "DUCK":
                document.write("The Duck Says QUACK QUACK");
                break;
        case "ROOSTER":
                document.write("The Rooster Says COC-A-DOODLE-DOO");
                break;
        default:
                document.write("The " + animal + " is silent.");
}
```

If the value on the associated "case" statement matches the value of the variable, the program executes the set of statements following the colon (:) character. If no matches are made, the program executes the code following the "default" statement. Note that each "case" block ends with a "break" statement. This causes program flow to exit the "switch" block, and turns control over to the statement immediately after the closing curly bracket.

The "for" statement is used to repeat a set of statements until the value of a defined variable reaches a specified value. The JavaScript syntax of the "for" statement is shown below:

```
for (variable initialization; comparison; incrementing expression)
{
}
```

The "variable initialization" value defines a variable that controls the "for" loop and its initial value. The "comparison" expression determines when the "for" loop is complete. Finally, the "incrementing expression" defines how the control variable should be incremented.

The following example illustrates the use of the "for" statement:

```
for (var x = 1; x < 10; x++) {
        document.write(myArr[x]);
}
```

This statement initializes the variable x to a value of one. The comparison expression tells the loop to continue execution as long as x is less than 10. The incrementing expression "x++" causes the value of x to be increased by one each time through the loop. The statement within the loop, which is executed with each iteration of the loop, displays the value of each element in the array myArr.

Similarly, you could create a "for" statement that worked in reverse order, as shown:

```
for (var x = 10; x > 0; x-) {
        document.write(x + "<br>");
}
```

In this example, the variable x is initially set to 10. The loop continues to execute as long as x is greater than zero. With each iteration, the value of x is decreased by one. It's important to note that the incrementing expression in the previous example and the decrementing expression in this example are both executed at the end of the loop. In this example, that means that the first time through the loop, x is 10 because it will not be decremented until the end of the loop.

Similarly, the "for...in" statement can be used to iterate through all of the elements in an array or all of the properties in an object. The example below illustrates the use of the "for...in" statement with an object:

```
for (var x in document) {
        document.write(x + " " + document[x] + "<br>");
}
```

This example uses the variable x to read each property associated with the "document" object. The statements inside of the curly brackets are executed for each property. The document .write() statement displays the property name stored in x and the property value accessed through document[x]. When executed in a browser, this script displays detailed information about the HTML document in which it is contained, as shown in Figure 3.5. In this example, the name of each available property is displayed, along with its value.

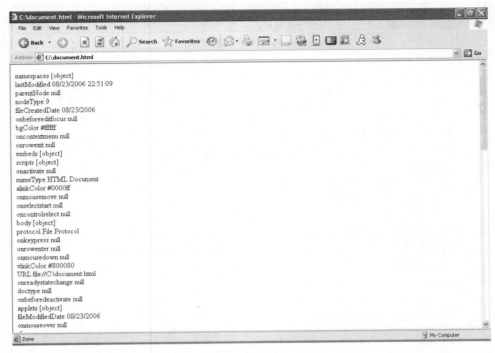

Figure 3.5: Object properties can be accessed using the "for...in" statement.

The "while" and "do...while" statements continue to execute a loop as long as a defined condition is true. The primary difference between these two statements is when the defined condition is tested. The "while" statement checks the condition at the beginning of the loop, so if the condition is false, the loop is never executed. Here is a basic "while" statement:

```
var x = 0;

while (x < 32) {
document.write(x);
x++;
}
```

In this example, every value from zero through 31 is displayed to the browser. Once the value reaches 32, the loop is exited.

The following example replaces the "while" statement with a "do...while" loop:

```
var x = 0;

do {
document.write(x);
x++;
} while (x < 32)
```

Note that the "while" condition appears at the end of the loop, and that's when the condition is actually tested. Therefore, every value is displayed from zero through 32.

Although the "while" and "do…while" statements perform similar functions, they serve distinct purposes. If the statements within the loop should never be performed when the defined condition does not exist, use the "while" statement. If, on the other hand, a calculation required as part of the conditional expression is performed within the loop, the "do…while" statement makes more sense.

The "with" statement is a convenience that lets you refer to the properties and methods of a given object without referencing that object over and over again. The two code fragments in the sample below illustrate the benefit of using this statement:

```
// using "with"
with (document) {
        var x = all("myTable");
        write("rows = " + x.rows.length + "<br>");
        write("cols = " + x.rows(1).cells.length + "<br>");
}

// "with"out
        var x = document.all("myTable");
        document.write("rows = " + x.rows.length + "<br>");
        document.write("cols = " + x.rows(1).cells.length +
"<br>");
```

As you can see, code placed within the "with" loop doesn't need to reference the object by name; that object is assumed. While this simple example doesn't explicitly illustrate the potential savings in code complexity, I'm sure you can picture how that savings would be achieved.

Browser/Document Access

In chapter 1, you saw how the JavaScript "window" object can control the browser interface. Since this object is at the heart of everything that JavaScript does, it's important to understand everything about it. Using the "window" object, it's possible to obtain information about, set attributes of, and control the reaction to defined events that occur within the browser window. Note that, since the "window" object is the primary object in your JavaScript source, it is *assumed*. This means that any properties, objects, methods, or events associated with the "window" object can be accessed without specifying the *window.* portion of the statement.

The "window" object itself contains a set of properties used to access information about the browser window, such as its size and position. Table 3.3 lists these properties, along with their uses.

Several of the properties in Table 3.3 reference the *browser dialog window*. It's possible to open a dialog box whose source is based on a web page. This can be extremely useful in creating a browser-based application because it lets you build more standard-looking customer dialog boxes that interact with the web application. For example, the source shown below could be used to adjust attributes of a browser dialog box:

```
<script language="JavaScript">
dialogHeight="200px";
window.dialogWidth = "400px";
dialogLeft="100";
dialogTop="400";
</script>
```

This code sets the height of the dialog box to 200 pixels and the width to 400 pixels. The dialog box is then moved to a position 100 pixels from the left side of the screen and 400 pixels from the top of the screen. Note that the "window" object is referenced explicitly once, while it is implied for the remaining three properties. This is done purely to illustrate that there is no difference between the two methods. The screenTop and screenLeft parameters also let you modify the location of a browser window relative to the screen.

Table 3.3: Properties of the "window" Object

Property	Description
closed	This property returns a Boolean value that identifies whether or not a specific window has been closed.
defaultStatus	This property is used to access the information displayed in the status bar once the document loads.
dialogArguments	This property is used to retrieve variables passed into a browser dialog window.
dialogHeight	This property reads and updates the height of a browser dialog window.
DialogLeft	This property reads and updates the leftmost coordinate of a browser dialog window.
DialogTop	This property reads and updates the top coordinate of a browser dialog window.
DialogWidth	This property reads and updates the width of a browser dialog window.
length	This property identifies the number of frames within the window object.
name	This sets or reads the name of the window object.
offscreenBuffering	This Boolean value identifies whether or not the window is generated off-screen before displaying to the user.
opener	This property is used as a reference to the window that opened the current window.
parent	This property identifies the parent of the current window.
returnValue	This property defines a return value from a browser dialog window to the main browser window.
screenLeft	This is the leftmost position of the browser window relative to the screen.
screenTop	This is the top position of the browser window relative to the screen.
self	This property is used to reference the current window.
status	This property is used to read or update the status bar's text for the browser window.
Top	This property is used to identify the uppermost parent window to the current window.

Several properties can be used to obtain information about other windows related to the current window. The "closed" property, for example, returns a Boolean value that identifies whether or not the defined window has been closed. This can be used from a parent window to determine if a child window has been closed, as shown here:

```
<script language="JavaScript">
var childWin = window.open("childwindow.html");

while (childWin.closed == false) {
// wait until child window is closed
}

// continue processing
document.write("DONE!");
</script>
```

This example creates a new child window and stores a reference to that window in the object childWin. Next, the "while" statement is used to stop processing within the current window until the child window is closed. Once the child window is closed, the message "DONE!" is displayed in the parent window. In applications like this one, where a parent window launches a child, multiple parent/child levels might be created. In these circumstances, you can access the highest-level parent using the "top" property on a given "window" object.

Browser dialog windows allow a programmer to display an HTML document as a standard dialog box. When using a browser dialog, however, you need a way to pass values back and forth between the parent window and the dialog window. Two properties allow you to do this. The dialogArguments property retrieves values that have been passed into the page. The returnValue property allows the page displayed in the dialog window to pass values back to the parent.

The "window" object also supports a set of event handlers that can be used to define an activity to be performed based on an event. Table 3.4 lists these event handlers, along with their uses.

Table 3.4: Event Handlers Associated with the "window" Object	
Event	**Description**
onblur	This event handler defines an action to be performed when the window is no longer in focus.
onerror	This event handler defines an action to be performed when an error event occurs within the browser window.
onfocus	This event handler defines the action to perform when the window gains focus.
onload	This event handler defines the action to perform when the window initially loads.
onresize	This event handler defines the action to be performed when the window is resized.
onunload	This event handler defines the action to perform when the window "unloads" before closing.

As you can see, these event handlers give you greater control over the user interface by controlling how your application responds to many events related to the browser window itself. These items are generally defined once within a web page, to associate any events that require control with a JavaScript function that will be used to obtain that control. The sample code below, for example, defines a function to be called for the onblur and onfocus events (whenever the window loses and gains focus):

```
<script Language="JavaScript">
window.onblur = blurEvt;
window.onfocus = focusEvt;

function blurEvt()
{
window.status="Sleeping...";
}

function focusEvt()
{
window.status="Ready!";
}
</script>
```

If a user switches to a different window than the one in which this script is defined, the status bar will display "Sleeping...." Once the user returns to this window, the status bar will change back to "Ready!" Generally, event handlers are within a script defined in the <head> section of the HTML document.

JavaScript also supports a robust set of methods to allow actions to be performed on the browser window, listed in Table 3.5. Although all of these actions are associated with the provided "window" object, many of them actually launch new windows or change the document displayed.

The alert(), confirm(), and prompt() methods all display a message in a dialog box. The main difference between the alert() and confirm() methods is that while alert() displays the message with only an OK button, confirm() displays both OK and Cancel buttons. This gives the programmer the ability to control the flow of a script based on the response received. The prompt() method also displays both OK and Cancel buttons, but adds a prompt for the user to enter a value and returns that value to the script. Here is a sample using each of these methods:

```
<script language="JavaScript">
var resp = window.prompt("Enter your name");

window.alert(resp + ", this is an informational message");

var conf = window.confirm(resp + ", do you want to continue?");

if (conf == false) {
window.close();
}
</script>
```

This script first displays a prompt requesting the user to enter his or her name. Next, an information dialog box is displayed, using the value returned from the prompt() method. Finally, the confirm() method is used to ask whether the user wishes to continue. The value returned by this method will be true if OK was clicked, and false if Cancel was clicked. If Cancel was clicked, the window is closed.

Table 3.5: Methods to Perform Actions on a Browser Window

Method	Description
alert()	This method displays a simple dialog box with a specified message. The dialog box only displays an OK button.
blur()	This method takes focus away from the current window.
clearInterval()	This method clears a timeout set using setInterval().
clearTimeout()	This method clears a timeout set using setTimeout().
close()	This method closes the window.
confirm()	This method displays a simple dialog box with a specified message. The dialog box displays OK and Cancel buttons.
createPopup()	This method creates a new pop-up window.
focus()	This method puts the window in focus.
moveBy(x,y)	This method moves the window by a specified number of pixels.
moveTo(*left,top*)	This method moves the window to the location identified by the left and top values.
Navigate(*url location*)	This method navigates to the URL supplied.
open()	This method opens a new browser window.
print()	This method sends the contents of the browser window to the printer.
prompt()	This method displays a dialog box that prompts the user to enter a response.
resizeBy()	This method resizes the window by a specified number of pixels.
resizeTo()	This method resizes the window to a specific width and height.
scrollBy()	This method scrolls the content by the specified number of pixels.
scrollTo()	This method scrolls the content to the specified coordinates.
SetInterval(*action, interval*)	This method performs a specified task every time the number of milliseconds specified on the interval parameter has passed.
setTimeout()	This method performs a specified task after the provided number of milliseconds has passed.
showModalDialog(*url, options*)	This method displays the supplied URL in a modal dialog box.
ShowModelessDialog (*url, options*)	This method displays the supplied URL in a modeless dialog box.

The open() and navigate() methods both load a new document, but navigate() reuses the existing browser window, while open() is generally used to display the document in a new browser window. Here is the syntax used with the open() method:

```
window.open(url, window_name, options, replace history)
```

In this statement, "url" represents a string containing the location of the URL to be opened. The "window_name" value identifies the window in which the document should be displayed. If an existing window name is used, the document is displayed in that window. Alternately, the value "_blank" can be used to indicate that the document should be displayed in a new window, or the value "_self" can be used to force the document to be displayed in the current window.

The "options" value represents a string containing a list of options related to the window itself. These options allow you to define the size, position, and look of the browser window by controlling whether or not title, menu, status, and/or tool bars are displayed. Table 3.6 lists commonly used options and their possible values.

The example below uses several options to display the desired document in a pop-up window:

```
window.open("mypopup.html", "_blank",
"height=200,width=400,status=no,toolbar=no,menubar=no,location=no")
;
```

This example identifies the height and width for the window, along with defining that the status bar, toolbar, menu bar, and location bar should *not* be displayed when the new window is opened.

The final optional parameter on the window.open() method is "replace history." It is used to identify whether or not the URL opened should replace the current URL in the browser history. Values of "true" and "false" are valid for this parameter.

...ied on the "open" Method

Option	Values	Description
		is option determines whether or not to display the window in ...lscreen mode.
		is option is used to define the height in pixels of the window.
		is option is used to define the leftmost corner in pixels for the ...t side of window.
		is option determines whether or not to display the location ...r containing the page URL.
		is option determines whether or not to display the browser's ...nu bar.
resizable	Yes/No	This option determines whether or not the window should be resizable.
scrollbars	Yes/No	This option controls whether or not scroll bars are displayed.
status	Yes/No	This option controls whether or not the status bar should be displayed.
titlebar	Yes/No	This option controls whether or not the title bar should be displayed.
toolbar	Yes/No	This option controls whether or not the toolbar should be displayed.
top	Number	This option defines the upper corner position of the top of the browser window, in pixels.
width	Number	This option defines the width in pixels of the browser window.

The window.navigate() method is very similar to window.open(), in that it is used to load a new document. While window.open() can be used to open a document in a new window, window.navigate() only loads the page into the current browser window. The example below uses window.navigate() to load the document "mainpage.asp" into the current browser window:

```
window.navigate("mainpage.asp");
```

As you might imagine, the window.close() method closes the defined window. This method can be used to close the current window or another window by associating that window with an object, as might be done using the "parent" or "opener" property.

The example below closes the window that opened the current window:

```
var opnrWin = window.opener;
opnrWin.close();
```

Note that security settings within the browser might cause a warning to be displayed prior to closing the browser window when window.close() is used. This example also helps to illustrate how all of the events, methods, and properties associated with the "window" object can also be accessed for another window.

The window.print() method allows you to send the contents of the browser window to the printer without having the user select the browser's print option. This can be valuable when you want to customize the user interface to an extent where the menu bar and toolbar are not displayed. The example below assigns this method to the "onclick" event for a button:

```
<input type="button" value="Print" onclick="window.print();">
```

When a user clicks the command button created by this statement, the web browser's print functionality is triggered. The action performed is exactly as though the user clicked "Print" from the "File" menu.

The "window" object also supports several methods that can be used to control time-triggered events. The setTimeout() and setInterval() methods are each used to identify a task to perform based on a specified elapsed time. The primary difference between the two methods is that while setTimeout() performs the specified action only once, setInterval() performs a specified action repeatedly while allowing the amount of time specified to elapse between each execution of the action. The following two statements illustrate the use of these two methods:

```
timeout = window.setTimeout(myFunction, 3000);

interval = window.setInterval(myTimer, 1000);
```

In each of these statements, the first parameter used with the method indicates the function to be executed. The second parameter indicates the delay, in milliseconds. In the case of setTimeout(), this delay takes place before the single execution of the defined function. With the setInterval() method, this is the delay that occurs between executions of the defined function. The activity scheduled by each of these methods can be cancelled using the clearInterval() and clearTimeout() methods. Both of these methods accept a single parameter that is used to identify the timeout or interval to be cancelled. The lines below would cancel the timeout and interval set in the previous example:

```
window.clearTimeout(timeout);

window.clearInterval(interval);
```

The clearTimeout() value can be used for situations where a delayed event has been initiated, but the web page includes a Cancel button to allow a user to cancel that functionality prior to its execution.

To control whether or not a given browser window holds focus, use the window.blur() and window.focus() methods. This functionality is particularly useful in controlling the display of child windows from a parent window, as shown here:

```
<script language="JavaScript">
var childWin1 = window.open("childwindow.html");
var childWin2 = window.open("childwindow2.html");

childWin2.blur();
childWin1.focus();


</script>
```

This example opens two new child browser windows and displays a unique web page in each one. Since childWin2 is opened last, it will initially have focus. The childWin2.blur() statement removes focus from that window. Next, childWin1.setFocus() ensures that childWin1 received focus once childWin2 loses it.

The "window" object also contains a collection called "frames." This collection, which is basically an array of objects, contains an element for each named frame displayed within the browser window. The statements below illustrate the use of this collection:

```
var frms = window.frames;

for (var i = 0; i < frms.length; i++) {
  alert(frms[i].name};
}
```

This example assigns the "frames" collection to the internal object "frms." The "length" property is then used to determine how many objects are contained within the collection. Next, the name of each object from the "frms" collection is displayed in a message. The document displayed in each frame within the "frames" collection can be accessed via the "document" object, which is one of several sub-objects of the "window" object and is also a sub-object of the "frames" collection. Table 3.7 lists all the sub-objects of "window," along with descriptions.

Table 3.7: Objects Contained within the "window" Object	
Object	**Description**
document	This object is used to access the document displayed within the browser.
event	This object is used to access information about events occurring within the browser.
history	This object can be used to access URLs that the user accessed from within the parent browser window.
location	This object contains the current URL for the document displayed in the current window.
navigation	This object is used to access data related to the user's browser client.
Screen	This object is used to access data related to the user's display screen.

Each of these objects contains its own properties, methods, and events. Because of this, we'll examine each object individually.

The "document" Object

This "sub-object" of the "window" object gives access to elements of the HTML document itself. In contrast, the "window" object controls the browser window in which that document is displayed. The properties associated with the "document" object are listed in Table 3.8.

Table 3.8: Properties of the "document" Object	
Property	**Description**
alinkColor	This property identifies the color of an active link within the document.
bgColor	This property reads or sets the background color for the document.
body	This property defines the document body.
cookie	This property is used to access cookies associated with the document.
domain	This property gets the server domain name for the document.
fgColor	This property reads or sets the foreground color for the document.
lastModified	This property returns a value indicating the date and time the document was last modified.
linkColor	This property reads or sets the color to be used for links within the document.
referrer	This property gets a value identifying the document that referred to the current document.
title	This property retrieves the title for the document.
url	This property retrieves the URL for the document.
vlinkColor	This property reads or sets the color for links in the document that were previously visited.

The document.alinkColor property, like several other "document" properties described here, reads or changes the color associated with links on the web page. In this case, the color relates to an active link on the web page, or a link that has been clicked but has not yet been displayed. The document.vlinkColor property identifies the color of a link that was previously visited. The simple document.linkColor property identifies the color of all other links on the page. Here are examples of setting each of these properties:

```
document.alinkColor = "Red";
document.vlinkColor = "White";
document.linkColor = "#0000FF";
```

The values supplied to these properties are the same ones that would be used in HTML. Similarly, the bgColor and fgColor properties read or change the background and foreground (font) color, respectively, as shown here:

```
document.bgColor = "Red";
document.fgColor = "White";
```

In this example, the background color for the page is set to red, and any fonts displayed within that page that don't have their own color definitions will be displayed in white.

In addition to these properties for setting colors, several properties give you access to information about the page itself. The document.domain, document.lastModified, document.referrer, document.title, and document.URL properties all contain information about the document itself. The document.domain property returns the domain name for the server hosting the document (*www.mc-store.com*, for example). The full uniform resource locator (URL) path to the document can be retrieved using the document.URL property. This value includes the full path to the document (*http://www.mc-store.com/index.html*, for example). The path to the document that linked to the current document is retrieved through the document.referrer property. As with the document.URL property, this property returns a fully qualified path, including any supplied "querystring" parameters. The document.title property returns the value defined in the page's <title> block. This value is generally displayed in the browser's title bar. Finally, the document.lastModified returns a date and time representing the last time the document was changed.

The document.cookie property gives you access to cookies stored on the computer displaying the page. *Cookies* are a means by which a programmer can store user-specific or system-specific data on a computer for later retrieval. Cookies are often used to store information like color preferences or user IDs, to make it easier to log in to commonly used web applications. The data related to a cookie is nothing more than a text file stored on a user's computer. The document.cookie property can be used to create a reference to the cookies related to a specific site. When creating a cookie, you must specify an expiration date and the path for which the cookie has value.

The script below gives an example of creating and retrieving a cookie using document.cookie:

```
<script language="JavaScript">
var date = new Date();
date.setTime(date.getTime()+(30*24*60*60*1000));
document.cookie = "Mycookie=FirstCookie; expires=" +
date.toGMTString() + "; path=/";

var cook = document.cookie.split(';');
for(var x=0; x < cook.length; x++) {
var c = cook[x];
        while (c.charAt(0)==' ') { c = c.substring(1,c.length);
}
                if (c.indexOf("Mycookie") == 0)
                document.write(c.substring(9,c.length));
}
</script>
```

This example creates a new cookie named MyCookie with a value of FirstCookie. The "expires" value represents the date and time when the cookie expires. The "path" value defines the path relative to the web server where this cookie is valid. Next, the example reads the cookie value back in, using the split() method to split the cookie based on the semicolon (;) character. This gives you access to each cookie associated with the path. The script then searches through the resulting array of cookies stored in the variable "cook" for a matching cookie name. When the name is matched, document.write() is used to write the value out to the browser window.

The document.body property is a means of accessing individual elements within the document body. These properties include aLink, link, vLink, bgColor and text, which are all used to control the colors used within the document. These are comparable to the similarly named properties you saw earlier. In addition to these, there are several other properties, including document.body.id, document.body.name, and document.body.innerHTML. The first two are directly relatable to their attribute counterparts on the <body> tag. The document.body.innerHTML property allows you to read and change the HTML contained within the document. The example below illustrates the use of this property to change what is displayed in the browser:

```
<html>
<body>
Hi!
</body>
<script>
document.body.innerHTML = "<p align='Center'>Hello World!</p>";
</script>
</html>
```

The body of this document contains the simple text "Hi!", but that will never be visible to the user. Instead, the script portion of the document changes the page to display the centered text "Hello World!" (Note that you can write out HTML tags right along with your text.)

It's also possible to access other individual web-page elements using the "document" object. These elements are accessed via a set of collections contained within the "document" object. Table 3.9 lists these collections.

Table 3.9: Collections Contained within the "document" Object	
Collection	Description
anchors	This collection contains all of the anchor (<a>) elements with a defined name.
applets	This collection is used to access all of the applet objects (<object> tags) within the document body.
forms	This collection gives access to all of the <form> objects within the document body, and all of the elements within those forms.
images	This collection contains all of the images (<img> tags) within the document body.
links	This collection is used to access all of the HTML hyperlink elements.

You access an individual element within any of these collections by name or numerically, as shown in the sample page here:

```
<html>

<body>
<img name = "Thing1">
<img name = "Thing2">
</body>

<script Language="JavaScript">
var imgs = document.images;

imgs(0).src = "image1.jpeg";
imgs("Thing2").src = "image2.jpeg";
</script>

</html>
```

In this example, the two <img> elements are created without image sources. JavaScript assigns the document.images collection to the variable "imgs." The first occurrence of the collection is accessed using the numeric identifier (0). The second sample accesses the image element using the name assigned to the element.

The "forms" collection not only gives access to an individual HTML form, but all of the items contained within the form, as well. Through this collection, it's possible to read and modify values entered into a form for validation purposes, or even to create new form elements. The page here illustrates these possibilities:

```
<html>
<head>
<script language = "JavaScript">
function login() {
        var frm=document.forms("MyForm");

        if (frm.elements("user").value == "") {
                alert("User Name Required");
                return(false);
        }

frm.elements("submitButton").value="OK!";

        var currDate = new Date();
        var oLoginTime = document.createElement("input");
```

```
                    oLoginTime.type = "hidden";

                    oLoginTime.name = "loginTime";
                    oLoginTime.value = currDate.getTime();
                    frm.appendChild(oLoginTime);

    }
    </script>
    </head>
    <body>
    <form name="MyForm" onsubmit="login();">
    <input type = "text" name = "user">
    <input type = "submit" name = "submitbutton" value = "Login">
    </form>
    </body>
    </html>
```

This example creates a simple HTML log-in form, with an input text box and a Submit button. The onSubmit event for the form points to the function login(). This event occurs when a user clicks the form's Submit button prior to actually sending the form to the server. The login() function checks to ensure that the user has entered a value in the user box. If not, an error message is displayed. Next, the value of the Submit button is changed to "OK!" Finally, a new form element is added. This is a hidden input box that holds the value of the current time.

Note that the new element is created under the "document" domain, and the appendChild() method adds the hidden element to the form. If you didn't do this, the value wouldn't be submitted to the server along with the form. This type of manipulation can also be used to add or remove form fields that depend on specific values in other form fields.

Document Object Methods

The "document" object also supports a set of methods to allow you to perform actions. Table 3.10 lists the methods supported by this object.

Table 3.10: Methods Used with the "document" Object	
Method	**Description**
clear()	This method removes all child elements in the document.
close()	This method closes an output data stream and displays the resulting data.
createAttribute(attrName)	This method creates a new attribute.
CreateElement(html tag)	This method creates a new child document element.
CreateTextNode(text string)	This method creates a simple text string
focus()	This method places the document in focus
getElementById(id)	This method allows access to specific document elements based on the element's ID attribute.
getElementsByName(name)	This method gives access to a collection of specific document elements based on the "name" attribute.
GetElementsByTagName(tag name)	This method accesses a collection of elements based on the tag name.
open()	This method opens a document for writing.
write(string)	This method writes a string of text to the document.
writeln(string)	This method writes a string of text to the document, followed by a line feed. It is used with document.open().

The document.open() method indicates that the current document should be cleared and replaced by a new document. The document.write() method is then used to stream the output to the new document. Finally, the document.close() method indicates that all output has been written out, and the document is complete. The following example illustrates each of these methods:

```
<html>
<head>
<script>
function docMethods()
{
var newDoc=document.open("text/html","replace")
var txt="<html><body>New Window content!</body></html>"
newDoc.write(txt)
newDoc.close()
}
</script>
</head><body>
<input type="button" value="click here to test "
onclick="docMethods()">
</body></html>
```

The document.clear() method initializes the contents of an object created using the document.open() method. This gives you the ability to remove elements before the document.close() method is executed. These three methods, along with document.write() and document.writeln(), give you the ability to output custom page elements on the fly, all from within JavaScript. Both document.write() and document.writeln() write HTML output to the document, but document.writeln() method also automatically appends a line-feed character to the end of the line.

Summary

It's easy to see how the JavaScript language allows you to dynamically add, remove, and change web page elements. Now that you've gained an understanding of the JavaScript language itself, in chapter 4, you'll explore a component of dynamic web-page design that goes hand-in-hand with JavaScript: cascading style sheets.

Cascading Style Sheets

HTML styles were introduced with HTML 4.0. Styles let you define how each element appears within a web page. Attributes like colors, fonts, and borders can be controlled through the use of styles. Styles are generally stored inside a *style sheet*. A style sheet can be defined either internally within the <head> element of the HTML page itself, or in an external ".css" file. Multiple external style sheets can be used within a single HTML page, giving the ability to break style-sheet definitions into reusable "modules" to be used in different parts of the HTML document.

The term *cascading style sheets* refers to the ability to define HTML element styles at multiple levels. This hierarchical approach allows generic styles to be overridden by specific HTML elements. The "cascading" hierarchy of styles is executed in the following order:

1. Default settings for the browser
2. External CSS style sheet definition
3. Internal CSS style sheet defined within the <head> element
4. Style defined within individual HTML elements

Styles defined at lower levels override those defined at higher levels. Style information on an HTML element, for example, will always override style information defined within an internal or external style sheet. Before we review the elements of style definition, let's examine how styles are defined using each of these methods.

Default/External Style Sheet

We'll examine default and external style sheets together because the default style sheet is simply an external style sheet that has been linked to the browser, to be used when no specific style definition exists. Within Internet Explorer, this link is defined from within the "Internet Options" dialog by clicking on "Accessibility" and selecting the "Format documents using my style sheet" checkbox. You supply the name of the file containing the external style sheet in the "Style sheet" field, as shown in Figure 4.1. The value specified in this field can be any external CSS file.

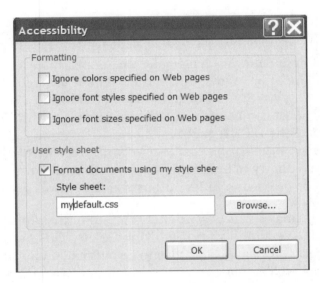

Figure 4.1: This dialog box is used to define the default style sheet in Internet Explorer.

External style sheets contain the same type of information that would be provided on an internal style sheet or an HTML element using the "style" attribute. To include an external CSS definition inside of an HTML web page, use the <link> element and specify the "href" attribute, as shown here:

```
<link href="mystylesheet.css" rel="stylesheet" type="text/css"/>
```

This statement indicates that the external style sheet named "mystylesheet.css" should be loaded and used for this web page.

Only those elements with style definitions within that external style sheet will be affected by this. For that reason, multiple <link> elements can be specified within a single HTML page. When multiple <link> elements are specified, the first one takes precedence over the second, which takes precedence over the third, and so on. The attribute *rel="stylesheet"* specified here indicates an external style sheet. It's also possible to specify "alternate style sheet," to identify an alternative style sheet that can be used based on user selection. You'll learn more about switching style sheets a little later in this chapter.

Internal Style Sheet

Internal style sheet definitions let you incorporate style definitions directly into your HTML. This can be useful when you want to override settings in the default CSS or an external CSS for specific elements of your web page. Internal style sheets are defined using the <style> element within the <head> section of an HTML document, as shown here:

```
<head>
 <style type="text/css">
   body {background-color:BLUE; color:RED; text-align: center}
 </style>
 </head>
```

In this example, the <style> element is used to define the background color, font color, and text alignment for the body of this HTML document. The biggest drawback to using internally defined style sheets is that they become specific to the page in which they are contained.

As mentioned earlier, it's possible to combine external style sheets with internal definitions, giving you the ability to use a standard style definition and override it as needed. The following source illustrates this:

```
<head>
 <link href="standard.css" rel="stylesheet" type="text/css"/>
 <style type="text/css">
   td {background-color:Yellow; color:Black; text-align: center}
 </style>
 </head>
```

This example derives most of its style information from the external style sheet file "standards.css." Within this page, however, the <td> elements will have their "background-color," "color," and "text-align" attributes overridden. This page-specific override will be in effect for all <td> elements in this page. You can also override specific elements within the page.

Inline HTML Style Definition

So far, you've seen how to define style information globally for your browser, using external style sheets, and using internal style sheets. It's also possible to override style information for individual elements within a web page. This capability is achieved through the "style" attribute. Most HTML elements support the "style" attribute.

The following lines of code use this attribute on several different HTML elements:

```
<p style="color:red; text-align:center;">My Text</p>
<table style="color:Blue;
border-style:solid;"><tr><td>Data</td></tr></table>
<input type="text" style="background-color:Orange;" name="textbox">
```

In this example, the <p> element is defined as having red text, centered within the document. The <table> element is defined as having blue text and a solid border around the table. With the <input> element, the resulting text box is displayed with an orange background.

As you can see, the style properties are defined in the format *property-name: property value*. Also, notice that multiple properties can be specified by separating them with semicolons (;).

As mentioned earlier, the concept of cascading style sheets means that higher-level definitions can be overridden at a lower level. The example below combines the previous two examples to help illustrate this:

```
<head>
 <link href="standard.css" rel="stylesheet" type="text/css"/>
 <style type="text/css">
    td {background-color:Yellow; color:Black; text-align: center}
 </style>
</head>
<body>
   <p style="color:red; text-align:center;">My Text</p>
   <table style="color:Blue; border-style:solid;">
   <tr><td>Data</td></tr></table>
   <input type="text"
          style="background-color:Orange;" name="textbox">
</body>
```

Within this page, any style properties defined in "standard.css" are applied to the page, with the exception of any <td> elements. These elements use the style defined in the internal style sheet. The color:Black property defined within that internal style sheet is overridden by the specific table definition, which redefines this property as color:Blue.

Style Sheet Properties

Now that you've seen where to define style sheet properties, let's take a look at what style sheet properties exist, along with their uses.

Properties used to defined style elements within an HTML document can be broken down into a set of simple categories. Each of these categories affects a different aspect of the way the document appears to the user.

Background Properties

The background properties define the look of the background of a displayed HTML document. Table 4.1 lists these style sheet properties.

Table 4.1: Background Style Sheet Properties	
Property	**Description**
background	This property can be used to define any of the other background properties.
Background-attachment	This property identifies whether a defined background image is fixed or scrolls with the rest of the window. Possible values are "scroll" and "fixed." This property is used when the background-image is also specified.
background-color	The background color for the document is defined using this property. The value can be defined as a color name, an RGB value, or a hex color code.
background-image	This is used to define an image file to be displayed as the background for a defined HTML document.
Background-position	The position of a background image within the document is defined using this property. This value can be specified as a constant (top left, etc.), a percent of the page down and across from the top left corner (such as 10% or 25%), or a specific number of pixels down and across from the top left corner.
background-repeat	This value identifies whether or not a background image should be repeated throughout the document.

The generic "background" property can be used instead of the other specific values. For example, the following style sheet assignment would be perfectly acceptable:

```
body {
background: red url(image.jpeg) no-repeat top left
}
```

This example defines the background information for the HTML <body> element. The color is defined using the named color "red." A background image is defined using the url() modifier. The "no-repeat" value indicates that the background image should be displayed only once. The positional values "top" and "left" indicate that the image should be positioned in the upper-left corner of the document.

It's also possible to explicitly define individual background properties. The "background-color" property identifies a color to be displayed as the background of a given element. The format of the value used to define this property can be any of the following:

- **Color name:** These are English color names, such as "red," "blue," or "green."

- **RGB color value:** This is in the format *rgb(red value, green value, blue value)*, where each color value is a number between zero and 255.

- **Hexadecimal color code:** This is a six-digit hex (hexadecimal) value, where the first two digits represent the amount of red, the next two digits represent the amount of green, and the last two digits represent the amount of blue.

Which method you use is largely a matter of personal preference. For example, the following three color definitions would all result in a red background:

```
background-color: red
background-color: rgb(255, 0, 0)
background-color: #ff0000
```

The "background-image" property lets you define an image file to be displayed in the background of a defined element. The image file itself is identified using the url() modifier, with the name and path to the image file indicated in parentheses. You can also specify a value of "none" to indicate that no background image should be displayed. The example below illustrates the use of this property:

```
td {
background-image: url(logo.gif)
}
```

This example results in the image "logo.gif" being displayed as the background to any <td> elements within the document. It's important to note here that many elements can use the "background-color" and "background-image" properties. There are also several background properties that act as modifiers to the "background-image" property. The "background-attachment" property, for example, identifies whether or not a defined background image scrolls with the rest of the document. The two possible values for this property are "fixed," to identify that the image should not be scrolled with the rest of the page, or "scroll," to indicate that the image should scroll with the rest of the page. Here are two examples of defining this property:

```
<body style='background-image:url(back.gif);
background-attachement:fixed'>
...
<style type="text/css">
    body {
        background-image: url(image.gif);
        background-attachment: scroll;
    }
</script>
```

In the first example here, the style definition is made within the <body> element directly. A background image named "back.gif" is defined as a fixed image. In the second example, the background image definition is again associated with the body element, but this time, it's defined within a style sheet. The image "image.gif" will also scroll with the rest of the document.

In addition to being able to define whether or not the image scrolls, it's also possible to define the position of the background image within the page. This is accomplished through the "background-position" property. This property can be defined using constants defining the position relative to the page, a relative position expressed as a percentage of the page, or a position expressed in pixels relative to the top left corner of the page. The following lines illustrate each of these methods:

```
background-position: top left; //upper left corner
background-position: 10% 25%; //10% of the page down,
    25% of the page over
background-position: 75 45;  // 75 pixels down, 45 pixels over
```

Valid constants for vertical positioning are "top," "middle," or "bottom." For horizontal positioning, valid values are "left," "center," or "right." As illustrated in the lines here, the vertical and horizontal values can be combined. If a vertical value is specified with no horizontal value, "center" is assumed.

The "background-repeat" property identifies whether or not a background image is tiled if necessary to fill a space. The valid values for this property are "repeat" to indicate that the image should be tiled across the element, "repeat-x" to indicate that the image should be repeated horizontally across the element, "repeat-y" to repeat the image vertically, and "no-repeat" to indicate that the background image should appear only once.

Border Properties

Many HTML elements, such as tables, table cells, images and text boxes, support visible borders. Several CSS properties allow you to control how these borders are displayed. Table 4.2 lists these border properties.

Property	Description
Table 4.2: Border Style-Sheet Properties	
border	This property lets you set all border properties in a single declaration.
border-bottom	This property defines the bottom border for a specified element.
border-bottom-color	This property identifies the color of the bottom border.
border-bottom-style	This property identifies the style of the bottom border.
border-bottom-width	This property identifies the width of the bottom border.
border-color	This property identifies the color of all borders for the specified element.
border-left	This property defines all of the properties associated with the left border.
border-left-color	This property identifies the left border color.
border-left-style	This property identifies the style of the left border.
border-left-width	This property identifies the width of the left border.
border-right	This property defines all of the properties associated with the right border.
border-right-color	This property identifies the right border color.
border-right-style	This property identifies the style of the right border.
border-right-width	This property identifies the width of the right border.
border-style	This property defines the style for all four borders in a single declaration.

Table 4.2: Border Style-Sheet Properties	
Property	**Description**
border-top	This property defines all of the properties associated with the top border.
border-top-color	This property identifies the top border color.
border-top-style	This property identifies the style of the top border.
border-top-width	This property identifies the width of the top border.
border-width	This property defines the width for all four borders in a single declaration.

You might have noticed that there is a hierarchical structure to these properties. The simple "border" property can be used to define all of the attributes associated with the element border in a single declaration. The "border-left" property can be used to set all of the properties associated with the left border. The "border-left-color" property defines the color of the left border only. An example of the use of the "border" property is shown below:

```
table
{
border: thin dotted blue
}
```

In this example, all of the table's borders would have a thin width, a dotted style, and a blue color. Alternatively, the "border-bottom," "border-top," "border-left," and "border-right" properties could be used to define these same three properties for the specific border in question, as shown here:

```
td
{
border-top: thin solid gray;
border-left: thin solid gray;
border-bottom: medium solid black;
border-right: medium solid black;
}
```

This example declares that <td> elements will have borders with thin, solid, gray lines on the top and left, and medium-width, solid, black borders on the bottom and right. The result is a somewhat 3-D effect, as shown in Figure 4.2.

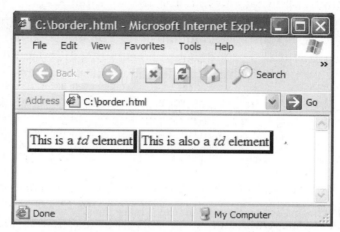

Figure 4.2: Defining border properties for table cells can give a 3-D effect.

It's also possible to define the specific portions of the border properties individually. The "border-color" property, for example, can be used to define all four border colors in a single declaration. Up to four color values can be specified with this property. These values can be either color names, RGB color values, or hexadecimal color codes. Here are three examples of defining border color using this property:

```
p {
   border-color: red white blue yellow;
}

tr {
    border-color: black orange;
}

img {
    border-color: green;
}
```

The first example sets all four border colors individually, starting at the top and going clockwise, so the top border is red, the right border is white, the bottom border is blue, and the left border is yellow. The second example uses only two colors. The first value identifies the color for the top and bottom borders, and the second value defines the color for the left and right borders. (To define an individual border color, use a property such as "border-left-color.") When defining any of the "border color" parameters, it's also possible to use the constant "transparent" to indicate that no border should be generated. In that case, whatever coloring is "behind" the element will be visible.

The "border-style" and "border-width properties" can be used to define the style and width for all four borders in a single declaration. Here are examples of each of these:

```
table {border-style: dotted dashed
border-width: thin medium}

tr {border-style: dotted dashed inset double
border-width: 3 4 5 6}

td {border-style: groove
thick}
```

The first example defines the top and bottom table borders as thin dotted lines and the left and right borders as dashed medium-width lines. The second example defines each border for table rows individually. Note that the widths here are pixels instead of constants. The final example defines a thick, 3-D grooved border style for <td>. In these examples, the "border-width" properties are defined using either a constant such as "thin" or a numeric pixel value. The "border-style" property is defined using one of the constants shown in Table 4.3.

Table 4.3: Possible Border Style Values	
Value	**Description**
none	No border is displayed.
hidden	As with "none," no border is displayed.
dotted	This value displays a dotted-line border.
dashed	This value displays a dashed-line border.
solid	This value displays a solid-line border.
double	This value displays a double-line border.
groove	A 3-D grooved border is displayed.
ridge	A ridged 3-D border is used.
inset	A border with an inset 3-D effect is displayed.
outset	A border with an outset 3-D effect is displayed.

Each of these border styles gives a unique effect to the HTML element with which it is used, as shown in Figure 4.3.

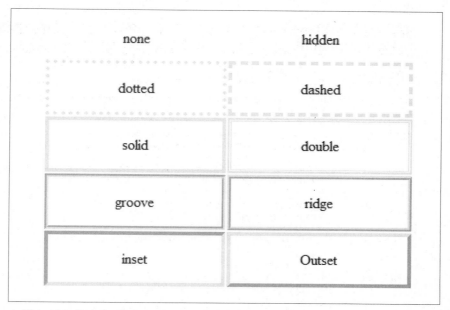

Figure 4.3: Each border style gives a different effect.

It's also possible to specifically define border property elements individually. For example, you could use the "border-left-color," "border-left-width," and "border-left-style" properties to individually define the properties associated with the left border, as shown in this example:

```
table {border-left-color: red;
       border-left-style: dotted;
       border-left-width: medium;}
```

This identifies that the left table border should have a medium-width, red, dotted line. It is equivalent to using "border-left: red dotted medium." Which method you choose to define the border properties depends on personal preference and the need you are attempting to meet. However, the use of specific property definitions is easier to read and understand.

Font Properties

The way text is displayed in HTML elements is controlled via the font properties. Table 4.4 lists these properties.

Table 4.4: CSS Font Properties	
Property	**Description**
font	This property lets you define all of the attributes of a font in one declaration.
font-family	This property lists the font family names to be applied to an element, in the order in which they should be applied.
font-size	This property defines the size of the font for a specified element, using a defined constant, a specified size, or a percentage.
font-style	This property defines font styling using one of the constants "none," "italic," or "oblique."
font-variant	This property indicates whether to display text in a small-caps font or a normal font.
font-weight	This property defines the font weight using a constant value ("normal," "bold," "bolder," "lighter") or a numeric value from 100 to 900.

As with the other CSS properties you've seen, the font properties let you define the same attributes at several different levels through different properties. The "font" property, for example, lets you define all font attributes in a single declaration, as shown below:

```
td
{
font: italic bold small-caps 12px arial
}
```

In this example, the text associated with all <td> elements will be displayed using Arial as the font, in a size of 12 pixels, with italic style, bold weight, and small caps.

You can also define fonts to match settings on the system, using a set of constant values. These font constants allow you to define the look of your web page to match that of the environment in which the page is displayed. This way, custom menus you create using CSS can match the look and feel that the user is used to. Table 4.5 lists these constants and their definitions.

Table 4.5: Font Constants	
Font Constant	**Description**
caption	Use the same font defined for captioned controls (radio buttons, drop downs, etc.).
icon	Use the same font as text displayed with icons.
menu	Use the same font displayed on window menus.
message-box	Use the same font displayed within message boxes.
status-bar	Use the same font displayed within the window's status bar.

The "font-family" property explicitly defines font names to be used with the specified element. The property accepts a list of fonts, which is applied in order from left to right. If the first font listed on the property does not exist on the client system, the next font will be used, and so on. The "font-size" property sets the size of the text font associated with the element. This property can be set using one of several constants, a specified size in points, or a percentage of the element containing the font. The constant values are listed in Table 4.6.

Table 4.6: Font-Size Constants

Font Size Constant	Description
xx-small	Use a double extra-small font size, based on the browser's font settings.
x-small	Use the extra small font.
Small	Display the font in the small font size.
Medium	Display the font using the medium font size.
Large	Display the font using the large font size.
x-large	Display the font using the extra-large font size.
xx-large	Display the font using the double extra-large font size.
smaller	Display the font one font size smaller than the current setting in effect.
larger	Display the font one font size larger than the current setting in effect.

The "font-style" property sets special font characteristics. The three possible options for this property are "normal," "italic," and "oblique." Similarly, the "font-variant" property further defines how the font is displayed. This property accepts two possible values: "normal" and "small-caps." The "small-caps" value indicates that lowercase letters should be displayed as smaller versions of the corresponding uppercase letters.

The final property for defining the look of the font is "font-weight." This property is used to control bold printing. Possible values for this property are the absolute values "normal" and "bold," or the relative values "bolder" and "lighter" to adjust the level of boldness relative to the current setting. It's also possible to use numeric values from 100 through 900, indicating the level of boldness. The lower values indicate lighter font thickness, while higher values indicate heavier thickness.

List Properties

List properties let you define text to be displayed as a bulleted list, along with defining the style of that bulleted list. Table 4.7 lists these properties.

Table 4.7: List Properties	
Property	**Description**
list-style	Use this property to set all of the list attributes.
list-style-image	This property defines an image file as the bullet for the list.
list-style-position	This property defines the location of the list marker. Possible values are "inside" and "outside."
list-style-type	This property defines the type of marker displayed with the list.

The "list-style" property defines all of the list's attributes in a single statement, as shown below:

```
{
   list-style: outside decimal
}
```

This example indicates that the list associated with the style should be decimal and numeric, with the list marker located in an outside position.

The "list-style-image" property indicates that an image file should be used as the list marker. The example below illustrates the use of this property:

```
{
   list-style-image: url(bullet.gif);
   list-style-type: disc;
}
```

In this case, the image file bullet.gif will be used as the list marker. Note that the "list-style-type" property also allows for the possibility that the list image is not available.

The "list-style-position" property identifies the location of the list item marker. A value of "inside" indicates that the marker should be left-justified relative to the list item's text. A value of "outside" leaves the list marker right-justified.

The "list-style-type" property, as you have already seen, defines the type of marker to be displayed with the list. This property lets you define if a simple bulleted list should be displayed, or if a numbered list should be used instead. Table 4.8 lists the available values for this property.

List Style Type	Description
Table 4.8: Possible List-Style-Type Values	
none	No list marker is displayed.
disc	A filled circle (disc) is displayed.
circle	An open circle is displayed.
square	A square is displayed.
decimal	Numbers are displayed.
decimal-leading-zero	Numbers with leading zeros are displayed.
lower-roman	Lowercase roman numerals are displayed.
upper-roman	Uppercase roman numerals are displayed.
lower-alpha	Lowercase letters are used for markers (a, b, c).
upper-alpha	Uppercase letters are used for markers (A, B, C).

These list properties define the style for the list tags <ul> and <li>. The example below illustrates the use of the "list-style-type" property within a <ul> tag:

```
<ul style="list-style-type: upper-roman; list-style-position:
outside;">
<li>First Item</li>
<li>Second Item</li>
<li>Third Item</li>
<li>Fourth Item</li>
</ul>
```

This example also incorporates the "list-style-position property" to cause the list marker to be right-justified. Figure 4.4 shows the output from this example.

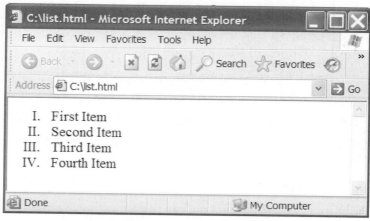

Figure 4.4: This list is generated using the list properties.

Margin Properties

To adjust the amount of space around an element, you can use the margin CSS properties. Five properties are available to define margins. These are shown in Table 4.9.

Table 4.9: Properties to Define Element Margins	
Property	**Description**
margin	This property sets all margins in a single definition.
margin-bottom	This property defines the bottom margin.
margin-left	This property defines the left margin.
margin-right	This property defines the right margin.
margin-top	This property defines the top margin.

For any of the margin-defining properties in Table 4.9, the value supplied should be either a numeric value representing pixels, a percentage representing the percent of the total page, or the constant value "auto" to allow the browser to adjust the margin automatically. It's also possible to define a negative value, which results in elements overlapping within the page.

If all four margins are to be the same, you can provide a single value. Alternatively, you can specify two values to define the top and bottom margins the same, and the right and left margins the same. If you want each of the four margins to be different, specify the values in the order top, right, bottom, and left. Below are examples of each of these scenarios:

```
{
margin: auto; // All four margins the same
margin: 8px 3%; // Top and bottom 8 pixels, left and right margins
at 3%
margin: 8px 7px 6px 5px; // Each margin defined individually
}
```

Padding Properties

While margin properties define the space between elements, padding properties define the space between an element's border and the content contained within the element. The best way to illustrate this is to look side-by-side at examples of padding and margins.

The source below defines two table cells, one with a three-pixel margin and the other with no margin, but a three-pixel padding:

```
<table><tr>
<td style='margin: 3px; border=2px'>Cell data</td>
<td style='margin: 0px; padding:3px; border:2px;'>Cell data</td>
</tr>
</table>
```

The first cell will have white space around its border. The second cell will have the white space between the border and the cell data. Figure 4.5 shows the resulting output.

As with the margin, padding attributes for all four sides of an element can be set using the "padding-bottom," "padding-left," "padding-right," and "padding-top" properties, or with the single "padding" property. Supported values for padding properties include a numeric pixel value

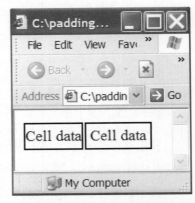

Figure 4.5: These cells illustrate margin versus padding.

or a value that represents a percentage of the total page size. Again, as with the "margin" property, the "padding" property can be set using a single value for all four sides, two values to identify the top and bottom as a pair and the left and right as another pair, or four values to define all four sides individually. The example below illustrates each of these scenarios:

```
{
padding: 3px; // all four sides
padding: 3px 2px; // top/bottom set to 3 pixels, left/right set to
2 pixels
padding: 2% 3% 1% 5%; // each side set individually
}
```

Text Properties

In addition to the font properties you saw earlier, there several other properties for defining the look of the text associated with an element. A list of these properties is shown in Table 4.10.

Table 4.10: Properties to Define How Text Is Displayed within an Element	
Property	**Description**
color	This property defines the text color.
direction	This property indicates whether text should be displayed right to left or left to right.
letter-spacing	This property defines the spacing between letters.
text-align	This property identifies how the text should be aligned relative to the element.
text-decoration	This property defines special text attributes, such as underlined or strike-through.
text-indent	This property defines indentation for the first text line in an element.
text-transform	This property allows you to transform the case of the supplied text.
white-space	This property defines how the white space within an element is handled relative to the text within the element.
word-spacing	This property defines the amount of spacing between words within an element.

The value of the "color" property can be supplied as an RGB() value, a hex code representation of a color, or one of the defined color constants supported by the browser. For example, in the following lines, the text in the first cell is displayed in red, the text in the second cell is black, and the text in the third cell is gray:

```
<td style="color:Red">Red Text</td>
<td style="color:#000000">Black Text</td>
<td style="color:rgb(128, 128, 128)Gray Text</td>
```

The "direction" property identifies the direction in which the text is displayed. Supported values for this property are "ltr" to indicate that the text is displayed from left to right, or "rtl" to indicate that the text should be displayed from right to left. The two lines below illustrate each scenario:

```
<td style="direction:rtl">backward</td>
<td style="direction:ltr">forward</td>
```

The text itself will appear as it is typed; however, it will be aligned according to the supplied value. Right-to-left alignment is used for languages normally read from right to left, like Arabic or Hebrew.

The "letter-spacing" property defines the spacing between letters. The value supplied should be either a numeric pixel value or the constant "normal" to identify that standard spacing for the defined font should be used. It's possible to define a negative value for this property, resulting in decreased spacing between characters. Both increased and decreased spacing are illustrated in this example:

```
<p style="letter-spacing:3px">Increased Spacing</p>
<p style="letter-spacing:-3px">Decreased Spacing</p>
```

The first line here increases the letter spacing by three pixels, while the second decreases that spacing by three pixels. Figure 4.6 shows the results of this example in the browser window.

The "text-align" property defines the alignment of text within an element. In addition to the values of "left," "center," "right," this property also supports "justify" to indicate that the text should fill the available space from left to right.

Figure 4.6: These two examples illustrate the "letter-spacing" property.

The "text-decoration" property indicates that certain special effects should be applied to the text. A list of the possible values for this property is shown in Table 4.11.

Table 4.11: Possible Values for the Text-Decoration Property	
Value	**Description**
Blink	The text blinks when displayed.
line-through	The text is displayed in a strikethrough style.
none	No decoration is applied.
Overline	A line is displayed above the text.
underline	A line is displayed under the text.

Figure 4.7: Here are the possible text-decoration styles.

Each of these possible values gives you the ability to further customize the look of text associated with a given element, as shown in Figure 4.7. (Note that the "blink" value is not supported by some browsers.)

The "text-indent" property defines the amount of indentation for the first line of text. The value provided can be a numeric value representing a number of pixels, or a percentage that identifies a percentage of the total width of the element. It's also possible to use a negative value on this property, causing the text to be shifted to the left, rather than indented to the right.

The "text-transform" property changes the case of the text. Possible values for this property include "capitalize" to change the first letter of each word to a capital letter and all others to lowercase, "lowercase" to convert all letters to lowercase, "none" to leave the text as-is, and "uppercase" to convert the text to all uppercase letters. The lines in the example below illustrate these values:

```
<p style="text-transform:capitalize">
The quick brown fox jumps over the lazy dog</p>
<p style="text-transform:lowercase">
The quick brown fox jumps over the lazy dog</p>
<p style="text-transform:none">
The quick brown fox jumps over the lazy dog</p>
<p style="text-transform:uppercase">
The quick brown fox jumps over the lazy dog</p>
```

The text enclosed within the <p> element is identical in each line, but the value of the "text-transform" property is different. Figure 4.8 shows the results of this example.

Figure 4.8: Using the "text-transform" property changes text case.

The "white-space" property defines how the browser should deal with white space within the element. Possible values are "normal" to identify that the browser should ignore white space, "pre" to leave the text spacing as-is in the same way that the <pre> tag does, and "nowrap" to identify that the text should not be wrapped within the element. Similarly, the "word-spacing" property lets you increase or decrease the amount of spacing between words within the element. The value "normal" on this property defines that the normal word spacing for the font should be used. A numeric value represents a fixed number of pixels to space between words. A negative value can also be used to decrease the amount of spacing between words.

CSS and JavaScript

The CSS properties discussed in this chapter allow you to create a very customizable user interface within a browser application. CSS properties go hand-in-hand with JavaScript, in that JavaScript can access and change any of these properties. Style-sheet properties are accessed from within JavaScript through the use of the JavaScript "style" object. This object gives full access to all of the style-sheet properties for a given element. Below is an example of using this function to change the background color of an HTML table cell (<td>) element with an ID of "td1":

```
<table><tr><td id="td1">Cell 1</td></tr></table>
<Script language="JavaScript">
var td1 = document.all("td1");
td1.style.backgroundColor = "Yellow";
</script>
```

This example illustrates the one difference between accessing a style-sheet property in CSS and accessing the same property in JavaScript. Inside of the JavaScript "style" object, capitalization takes the place of hyphens for multiple-word properties. For example, the CSS property "background-color" is replaced with "backgroundColor." Other than this difference in naming convention, all of the functionality explained in this chapter applies to defining values for style-sheet properties in JavaScript.

Summary

In this chapter, you saw how style-sheet properties can be used to customize the look of a web page. In the next chapter, you'll examine JavaScript function templates to perform common tasks. These function templates can be customized to meet your exact needs.

CHAPTER 5

JavaScript Functions

In chapter 3, you saw how to create custom JavaScript functions. In this chapter, you'll go a step further, taking a look at some useful functions that you can customize to suit your needs. These functions all handle common tasks required by browser-based applications. The examples in this chapter not only give you usable JavaScript functions, but also help to illustrate JavaScript programming techniques.

Form-Validation

One of the greatest features of JavaScript is its ability to validate HTML form data before posting that data to the server. This not only saves time, but also creates a cleaner user interface by giving instant feedback to the user when required data is invalid or missing, rather than having to reload the page from the server to show an error message. Validation functions are usually handled as part of the <form> element's onSubmit event. This event, which is fired prior to actually submitting the page to the server, lets you halt the submission of the form.

Here is a sample of a <form> element definition that includes the onSubmit event:

```
<form name="myForm" action="formhdl.asp" onsubmit="return
validate();">
```

In this example, the form "myForm" is defined to be submitted to the Active Server Page "formhdl.asp." Before submitting the form, the JavaScript function validate() is called. Note that the "return" method precedes the function name in the event definition. This causes the result of the function to be returned to the browser before submittal. If the function returns a value of "false," the page is not submitted. A value of "true" indicates that the form submission should continue.

Form validation can be as simple as checking to ensure that a given form field has a value, or as complex as checking for valid data based on defined criteria, or even checking an XML data source to ensure that a valid entry was made. To start off, let's examine a few basic form-field validation techniques and some functions that can be used to test values.

Required Fields

The simplest type of validation just ensures that a required field has an entry. This is literally the simplest validation because it only requires checking that a value is provided.

Figure 5.1 contains the source for the isBlanks() JavaScript function. This function loops through the value supplied in the inputvar variable, using the "\s" escape character to check that each character is blank. (A list of JavaScript escape characters can be found in the appendix of this book.) If a value other than blank is found, or if the value supplied is null, the function returns "false." Otherwise, "true" is returned to indicate that the field is blank.

```
function isBlanks(inputvar){
    if (inputvar != null){
        for(var x = 0 ; x<inputvar.length; x++) {
            if (inputvar.charAt(x)!='\s')
            {return false;}
            }
    return true;
    }
    else {
    return true;}
}
```

Figure 5.1: The isBlanks() function checks for an empty field value.

The isBlanks() function is contained within the JavaScript source file "jsfunctions.js," included in the downloadable code that is available with this book. To reference this source in your page, use a <script> block within the <head> element, as shown below:

```
<head>
    <script language="JavaScript" src="jsfunctions.js"></script>
</head>
```

Putting isBlanks() in the <head> element ensures that the function is loaded into the browser before there are any attempts to call it.

Figure 5.2 contains an HTML page that uses the isBlanks() function:

```
<html>
  <head>
    <script language="JavaScript" src="jsfunctions.js"></script>
    <script language="JavaScript">
        function validate() {
            var frm = document.all("myForm")
            if (isBlanks(frm.reqdField.value)) {
                alert("An Entry is Required");
                frm.reqdField.setFocus;
                return false;}
        }
    </script>
  </head>
  <body>
    <form name="myForm" onsubmit="return validate();">
        <input type="text" name="reqdField">
        <input type="submit" value="Submit">
    </form>
  </body>
</html>
```

Figure 5.2: This example uses the isBlanks() function.

This example uses the isBlanks() function in the validate() function, which has been associated with the onSubmit event for the form. Within the validate() function, the form named "myForm" is associated with the variable "frm." That association gives access to the elements within the form by the element's name value. The "if" statement determines whether or not the input box named "reqdField" has a value. If not, the alert() method displays a message to the user indicating that an entry is required. The setFocus method is also used to move focus to the field in error. Finally, the "if" statement executes "return false;" to indicate that the form should not be submitted to the browser. If an entry exists in this field, the form is submitted as expected.

Most of the time, simply checking that a field has a value is not enough. You'll also need to verify that the value of the field is what is expected. For example, you'll need to check that a numeric field doesn't contain alphanumeric characters. Figure 5.3 contains the source for more field-validation functions that can also be found in "jsfunctions.js."

```javascript
function isBlanks(inputVar){
    if (inputVar != null){
        for(var x = 0 ; x<inputVar.length; x++) {
            if (inputVar.charAt(x)!='\s')
            {return false;}
            }
    return true;}
    else {return true;}
}

function isNumeric(inputVar) {
    var numChars = "-.0123456789";
    if (inputVar != null){
        for(var x = 0 ; x<inputVar.length; x++) {
            if ((inputVar.charAt(x)!='\s') &&
            (numChars.indexOf(inputVar.charAt(x)) == -1)) {
            return false;
            }
        }
    return true;}
    else {return true;}
}

function isDate(inputVar) {
    var dateFmt = /^\d{1,2}\/\d{1,2}\/\d{4}$/
    if (dateFmt.test(inputVar)) {
        var dteArray = inputVar.split("/");
        var dte = new Date(inputVar);
        return dte.getMonth() + 1 == dteArray[0] && dte.getDate() ==
dteArray[1] && dte.getFullYear() == dteArray[2];
    }
    else {return false;}
}
```

Figure 5.3: These functions are used for form-field validation (part 1 of 2).

```
function isAlpha(inputVar) {
    var alphaLtrs =
        "abcdefghijklmnopqrstuvwxyzABCDEFGHIJKLMNOPQRSTUVWXYZ";
    if (inputVar != null){
            for(x=0;x<inputVar.length;x++) {
            if(alphaLtrs.indexOf(inputVar.charAt(x))==-1
        && inputVar.charAt(x)!='\s') {
                return false;
                }
    }
    return true;}
    else {return true;}
}
```

Figure 5.3: These functions are used for form-field validation (part 2 of 2).

In addition to the isBlanks() function, three other field-validation functions shown here. The isNumeric() function checks to ensure that a field contains only the digits 0 through 9, along with a decimal point or negative sign. This function validates numeric fields and ensures that the user hasn't entered invalid data into a numeric field. This is accomplished by comparing each character in the field supplied on the inputVar variable, using the indexOf() function. This function searches for a given character within a defined string. In this case, that defined string contains all of the acceptable characters for a numeric value. You can substring input value using the charAt() function. This extracts the character from the defined position within the variable. If the supplied variable contains numeric values only, the isNumeric() function returns "true"; otherwise, it returns "false."

Here is an example of the code required to use the isNumeric() function:

```
if (!isNumeric(frm.myField.value)) {
    alert('Numeric values only');
}
```

In this example, if the value of the field myField does not contain a valid numeric value, the message "Numeric Values Only" is displayed.

The isDate() function determines whether a supplied value is a valid date in the format *mm/dd/yyyy*. The function uses a string of control characters to determine if the supplied value matches the requested date format. The control character string "/^\d{1,2}\/\d{1,2}\/\d{4}$/" checks the supplied value for simple formatting. The control character "\d{1,2}" identifies that the first portion of the value should be a one- or two-digit number. The "\d{4}" control character identifies that the last portion of the variable should be a four-digit number. To perform a comparison using this string, isDate() uses the test() function on the input variable. If the simple formatting is okay, isDate() splits the input variable, using the "/" character as a delimiter. This allows you to break the date field into month, day, and year values. Next, it converts the input variable to a true date value using the Date() function. This JavaScript function accepts invalid dates, and adjusts them to a "best guess" of actual date. The returned date is broken into month, day, and year values according to the array elements containing the values split from the original input variable. If these values all match, the date entered is valid. If not, the user entered an invalid date.

It's important to note that this function explicitly validates only dates in the *mm* / *dd* / *yyyy* format. The function can be modified or extended to accept other formats. This function can be used not only for validation, but also to determine if the value provided can be converted to a date value reliably. The example below illustrates this:

```
if (isDate(frm.endDate.value)) {
    var trueDate = new Date(isDate);
    var currDate = new Date();
    if (trueDate > currDate) {
        alert('The end date must be less than the current date');
    }
}
else {
alert('The end date is invalid');
}
```

In this example, if the entered date is determined to be valid, the value is converted to a true date value using the Date data type. If the converted date value is greater than the current date, an error message is displayed. You'll also notice that this code returns an invalid date method if the value is determined to be invalid.

The isAlpha() function determines whether the supplied variable contains only letters *a* through *z* (uppercase or lowercase). This function uses a technique similar to that used in the isNumeric() function. The variable alphaLtrs is populated with the uppercase and lowercase versions of the alphabetic characters. The function loops through the input variable and uses the charAt() function to extract each character, then uses the indexOf() function to determine if the extracted character is contained within the alphaLtrs string. Once a non-alphabetic character is encountered, a value of "false" is returned by the function. The code below illustrates the use of this function:

```
if (!isAlpha(frm.firstName.value)) {
        alert('This field only accepts alphabetic characters');
        frm.firstName.setFocus;
        return false;
}
```

In this example, the firstName field is checked to determine if it contains anything other than alphabetic characters. If it does, an error message is returned to the user, and focus is moved to the field in question before returning "false" from the validation subroutine.

Each of the form-field validation functions in "jsfunctions.js" can be easily changed to fit any special needs you might have. For example, in addition to validating entire entries, it's also possible to prevent a user from entering data into a field that the field cannot support, such as entering a letter of the alphabet into a date field. You can restrict this by trapping the keyboard event on the input box related to the field, using the onKeyPress event along with the keyTrap() function included in "jsfunctions.js." Figure 5.4 contains the source for the simple keyTrap() function.

```
function keyTrap(validKeys, display) {
    var keyCd = window.event.keyCode
    if (!window.event.keyCode) keycode=window.event.which;
    var character=String.fromCharCode(keyCd);
    if (validKeys.indexOf(character) < 0) {
        if (display == true) alert("Invalid Entry");
        return false;
    }
    return true;
}
```

Figure 5.4: This function is used to restrict keyboard entries.

This function accepts a string parameter containing all of the valid characters to be keyed into this field, and a "true/false" value to identify whether or not to display an error message if the key pressed is invalid. The function uses both the window.event.keyCode and window.event.which properties to allow for maximum browser compatibility. These two properties return the key code associated with the keyboard event that caused the function to be called. This key code is converted to a character using the fromCharCode() method on a JavaScript String object. Next, the indexOf() function determines if the key pressed is found within the string provided on the function's validKeys parameter. If the entry is not found in that string, and the "display" parameter is "true," an error is displayed. If "false" is specified, or the second parameter is omitted, no error is displayed, but invalid key entries will not appear in the input box. This is accomplished by returning the value of "false" to the caller, instructing the browser not to pass the key to the input box. If the entry is found, a value of "true" is returned, and the key entry will appear in the field.

The source below illustrates how to associate the keyTrap() function with an input box:

```
<HTML>
    <HEAD>
    <TITLE>Key Trapping</TITLE>
        <script language="JavaScript"
src="jsfunctions.js"></script>
    </head>
```

```
    <body>
     <form name="myForm">
         <input type=text
        onkeypress="return keyTrap('0123456789/',false);"
 name="myKeys">
     </form>
    </body>
   </html>
```

In this example, the input box named "myKeys" accepts values of 0 through 9, along with the forward slash (/) character. The "false" value specified on the keyTrap() function's second parameter instructs the function to bypass the displaying of an error message. It simply prevents any invalid key presses from reaching the input box.

Form Control

In addition to validating data entered within an form, JavaScript functions also give you the ability to control the form itself by adding elements and even submitting the form. There are many circumstances where this ability is extremely valuable. Figure 5.5 contains a simple HTML log-in form, along with an onSubmit event function.

```
<script language="JavaScript">
function form_submit() {
    var frm = document.forms("loginForm");

    var currDate = new Date();
    var oLoginTime = document.createElement("input");
    oLoginTime.type = "hidden";
    oLoginTime.name = "loginTime";
    oLoginTime.value = currDate.getTime();
    frm.appendChild(oLoginTime);


}
</script>

<form name="loginForm" onsubmit="form_submit();">
    User: <input type="text" name="username"><br>
    Password:<input type="password" name="password"><br>
    <input type="submit" name="login" value="Login">
</form>
```

Figure 5.5: You can use a JavaScript function to append data to a form.

Prior to submitting the log-in form to the server, the onSubmit event launches the function form_submit(), which appends a hidden input field containing the time the form was submitted.

JavaScript functions can also be used to enable or disable fields and specific values based on selections made within the form itself. The example shown in Figure 5.6 illustrates this, using a form with two radio buttons.

```html
<html>
<head>
  <title></title>
<script language="javascript">
function showHide() {
    var srcEl = event.srcElement;
    var sel1 = document.getElementById("Select1");
    sel1.style.display = (srcEl.value == "1") ? '' : 'none';
}
</script>
</head>

<body>
  <form name="form">
    Favorite Color:</br>
    <input type="radio" name="choice" id="choice1" value="0"
      onclick="showHide();"/>I don't have a favorite color</br>
    <input type="radio" name="choice" id="choice2" value="1"
      onclick="showHide();"/>My Favorite color is:
    <select name="selectItem" style="display:none" ID="Select1" >
        <option >- Select a color -</option>
        <option>Red</option>
        <option >Blue</option>
        <option>Green</option>
        <option>Yellow</option>
        <option>Pink</option>
        <option>Purple</option>
    </select></br>
    </form>
  </body>
</html>
```

Figure 5.6: This page dynamically hides and displays form elements.

When this page is loaded in the browser, the list box created with the <select> element is only displayed if the second option button is selected. Otherwise, the list box is invisible. This is accomplished through the showHide() function, which has been associated with the onClick event for each of the radio buttons. The "display" style sheet property for the <select> element is initially set to "none," which causes the element to be invisible. When the second option button is selected, that value is changed to a blank string, which makes the element visible. Figure 5.7 shows how this works.

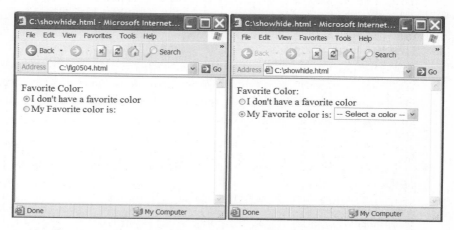

Figure 5.7: The "Select a color" list box is hidden or displayed dynamically using JavaScript.

As this example shows, it's very simple to dynamically change the contents of a form based on user input. This same technique can be used to dynamically change the layout and look of a browser page.

Dynamic Page Output

As you've seen in several examples already, JavaScript gives you the ability to easily and dynamically change elements within a page. One key component to this ability is the <div> element. This page element enables you to create logical groupings of other elements within a web page. Once you've created these groupings, you can show or hide them based on a user request or other event. The showHideDIV() function, which is in the JavaScript file "jsfunctions.js" included in the downloadable code available with this book, is shown in Figure 5.8.

```
function showHideDIV(divId) {
    var div = document.getElementById(divId);;
    if (div.style.display == "none") div.style.display = "";
    else div.style.display = "none";
}
```

Figure 5.8: The showHideDIV() function is used with <div> elements.

This function simply toggles the status of the "display" style property between "none" and blank. As a result, the <div> passed in the divId parameter will be hidden or displayed. Figure 5.9 shows a sample HTML document that makes use of this function, via the "jsfunctions.js" include file.

```
<html>
    <head>
        <script src="jsfunctions.js"></script>
    </head>
    <body>
        <a href="#" onclick="showHideDIV('section1');">Show/Hide
section 1</a>
        <div id="section1">
        <table border=1 width=100% height=40%>
          <tr><td width="95%">Section 1</td>
            </tr></table>
        </div></br>
        <a href="#" onclick="showHideDIV('section2');">Show/Hide
section 2</a>
        <div id="section2">
        <table border=1 width=100% height=40%>
          <tr><td width="95%">Section 2</td>
            </tr></table></br>
        </div>
    </body>
</html>
```

Figure 5.9: This HTML page uses the showHideDIV() function.

The page in Figure 5.9 has two <div> elements, each containing a one-cell HTML table. Preceding each <div> on the page is an <a> element containing an onClick event that calls the showHideDIV() function for that <div> element. When the page is initially displayed, both tables are visible. When a user clicks the "Show/Hide" link above the tables, the <div> associated with the link is hidden or shown. Note that when the top table is hidden, all of the space taken up by the table is compressed.

Figure 5.10 shows the results. As you can see, both sections are initially visible. When the "Show/Hide section 1" link is clicked, that section disappears and whatever appears directly below the <div> is moved up. Since this is a client-side JavaScript function, the item is hidden without reloading the page from the server. This is key, in that the data inside of the hidden <div> element is still there, it's just not visible.

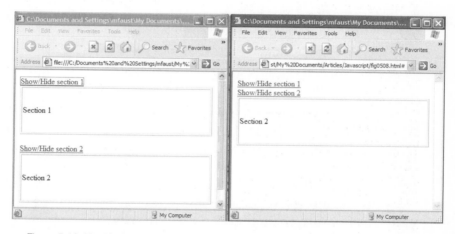

Figure 5.10: Here is the showHideDIV() function in action.

Another function inside of "jsfunctions.js" is moveDIV(divID, xPos, yPos). This JavaScript function accepts three parameters. The divID parameter identifies the ID property associated with the <div> to be moved. The xPos and yPos parameters identify the horizontal and vertical position to which the <div> should be moved.

Figure 5.11 contains the source for the moveDIV() function. This function can be used to move a <div> to a specified position, or optionally to move the <div> to the current mouse position. (You'll see how this could be used a little later in this chapter.)

```
function moveDIV(divId, xPos, yPos) {
  var div = document.getElementById(divId);
  div.style.position="absolute";
  if (xPos) {
     div.style.left=xPos;
  }
  else {
     div.style.left=getXMousePOS();
  }

  if (yPos) {
     div.style.top=yPos;
  }
  else {
     div.style.top=getYMousePOS();
  }
}
```

Figure 5.11: The moveDIV() function can be used to move a <div>.

This fairly simple function first retrieves a reference to the <div> identified on the divId parameter. The position of the <div> is handled through several style-sheet properties. First and foremost, the "position" property is changed to "absolute." This is done to ensure that the <div> is moveable. If this property is not "absolute," the <div> cannot be moved. If either the xPos or yPos values are omitted, the function assumes that the current mouse position should be used.

The vertical position is set using the "left" style-sheet property, while the horizontal position is set using the "top" style-sheet property. The mouse position values are retrieved using two other functions within the "jsfunctions.js" JavaScript source file. The getYMousePOS() function returns the horizontal mouse position within the screen, and the getXMousePOS() function returns the vertical position. The source for these two functions is shown in Figure 5.12.

```
function getXMousePOS() {
    if (document.layers) {
        // Netscape Specific code
        xMousePos = window.event.pageX;
    } else if (document.all) {
        // IE specific code
        xMousePos = window.event.x+document.body.scrollLeft;
    }
    return xMousePos;
}

function getYMousePOS() {
    if (document.layers) {
        // Netscape Specific code
        var yMousePos = window.event.pageY;
    } else if (document.all) {
        // IE specific code
        yMousePos = window.event.y+document.body.scrollTop;
    }
    return yMousePos;
}
```

Figure 5.12: These functions return the horizontal and vertical mouse positions.

Note that these two functions are written to support both Netscape and Internet Explorer browsers. The method used here is a common way to determine what browser is being used to display a document, by attempting to access an object that exists in one browser but not the other.

Figure 5.13 gives an example of the use of the moveDIV() function, accessed through the "jsfunctions.js" source file. The <div> with an ID of "myDiv" contains a small HTML table. Outside of the <div>, input fields exist to allow a user to enter an x and y position. There is also a command button that includes an onClick event to trigger the moveDIV() function.

```
<html>
  <head>
    <script language="JavaScript" src="jsfunctions.js">
    </script>
  </head>
  <body>
    <div id="myDiv"  width="100%" height="100%">
    <table style="background-color:red">
    <tr><td>Cell 1</td><td>Cell 2</td></tr>
    <tr><td>Cell 3</td><td>Cell 4</td></tr>
    <tr><td>Cell 5</td><td>Cell 6</td></tr>
    <tr><td>Cell 7</td><td>Cell 8</td></tr></table></div>
    X Position:<input type="text" name="xPos">
    Y Position:<input type="text" name="yPos">
    <input type="button" value="Move DIV"
        onclick="moveDIV('myDiv', xPos.value, yPos.value);">
  </body>
</html>
```

Figure 5.13: This page uses the moveDIV() function.

Figure 5.14 shows the results of the page. The table is initially located above the text. Once the moveDIV() function changes the "position" property to "absolute," the space containing the table is truncated. The <div> itself is moved to a new location based on the coordinates keyed into the supplied field.

Note that this position can overlay other information on the page, as it does here. If either of the coordinates is not supplied, the function moves the <div> to the current mouse pointer position.

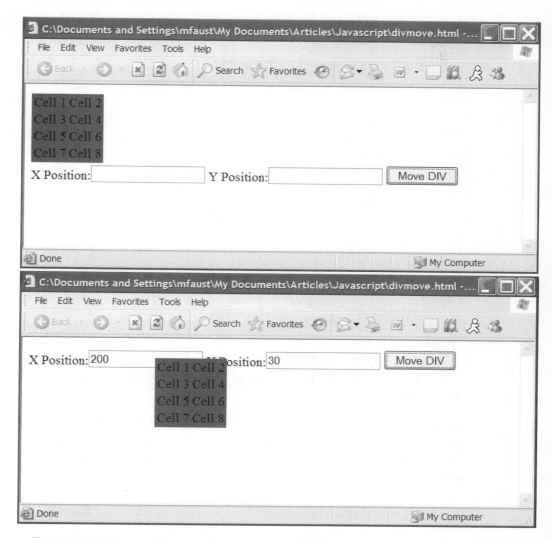

Figure 5.14: These two screens show the use of the moveDIV() function.

It's also possible to use this technique to create "drag-able" <div> elements within a page. Figure 5.15 contains three additional <div> functions that make this work.

```
var activeDIV = null;

function dragDIV() {
    moveDIV(activeDIV);
}

function activateDIV(divID) {
    if (document.onmousemove == null) {
        if (activeDIV == null) {
            activeDIV = divID;
        }
        document.onmousemove = dragDIV;
    }
}

function deactivateDIV() {
    activeDIV = null;
    document.onmousemove = null;

}
```

Figure 5.15: These functions allow users to "drag and drop" a <div>.

Note that the variable activeDIV in Figure 5.15 is defined outside of any functions, which makes it a global variable available to all functions. The activateDIV() function identifies the <div> element to be dragged and to trigger the document.onmousemove event. This event is associated with the dragDIV() function. That function simply calls the moveDIV() function for the <div> element that has been selected. You have to use this method, rather than associate the onmousemove event directly with the moveDIV function, because you can't use a function that requires parameters when making this type of association. The deactivateDIV() function removes the association with the onmousemove event and clears the "activeDIV" variable.

To see how to use these functions, look at the HTML source in Figure 5.16. In this example, the deactivateDIV() function is associated with the onmouseup event for the <body> element. The onmouseup event is fired when a user releases the mouse button. The function is associated with the event for the <body> element to ensure that the event is activated properly, no matter where the cursor is when the button is released.

```html
<html>
  <head>
    <script language="JavaScript" src="jsfunctions.js">
    </script>
  </head>
  <body onmouseup="deactivateDIV();">
    <div id="myDiv"  width="100%" height="100%" >
      <table style="border-width:thin ;background-color:menu">
      <tr style="background-color:ActiveBorder;cursor:hand;"
      onmousedown="activateDIV('myDiv');">
      <td colspan=2>Click to Drag</td></tr>
      <tr><td>Cell 1</td><td>Cell 2</td></tr>
      <tr><td>Cell 3</td><td>Cell 4</td></tr>
      <tr><td>Cell 5</td><td>Cell 6</td></tr>
      <tr><td>Cell 7</td><td>Cell 8</td></tr></table></div>
    </body>
</html>
```

Figure 5.16: This page uses a "drag-able" <div>.

The <div> named "myDIV" contains an HTML table that, when displayed, resembles a small window. The first row of the table is defined to resemble a title bar by using a different background color and changing the mouse cursor to the hand icon. Within this row, the onmousedown event is associated with the activateDIV() function for the <div> element. The result is that a user can click and drag this "pseudo-window" object around inside of the browser window. When the user releases the mouse button, the <div> remains in the spot where it was "dropped."

Figure 5.17 shows an example of the output displayed by this page. This example shows how you can extend the usefulness of the moveDIV() function by combining it with other functions. It also helps to illustrate the ability to capture events like mouse movements and make use of them within an application.

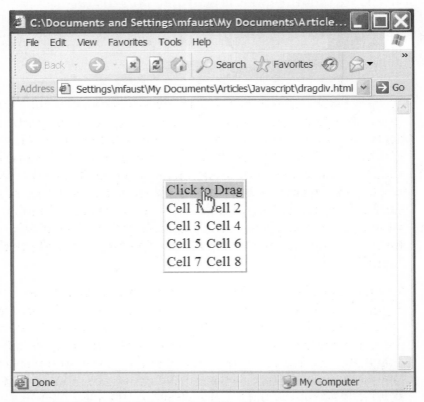

Figure 5.17: This example illustrates a drag-able <div>.

You can extend this example one step further by using the same type of functionality to create a context menu. This type of function can help give your application a more custom look and feel. Figure 5.18 shows the source for two more functions found within jsfunctions.js, which are used to accomplish this.

```
function dispMenu(menuID) {
    var menu = document.getElementById(menuID)
    moveDIV(menuID);
    menu.style.display="";
}

function hideMenu(menuID) {
    var menu = document.getElementById(menuID)
    menu.style.display="none";
}
```

Figure 5.18: These two functions are used to display and hide context menus.

While these two functions by themselves are somewhat unimpressive, when combined with some CSS functionality and a little bit of good old HTML, you can achieve a very nice effect. The dispMenu() function accepts a single parameter that represents the ID of the <div> containing a pop-up menu. This value is used with the moveDiv() function to locate the <div> at the cursor location. Finally, the "display" style property is set to blanks, which causes the hidden object to be displayed. The hideMenu() function reverses this, by setting the "display" property back to "none."

To understand how to use these functions, look at the example in Figure 5.19. In this case, a custom style sheet is defined, creating "class" definitions for the <table> and <td> elements. These class definitions allow you to create custom styles to be applied to specific elements. Here, a table class named "menu" defines the background color and border style of the context menu, and a td class named "menuitem" defines the font color and mouse pointer to be used for each item within the menu. Next, the "jsfunctions.js" JavaScript source file is associated, so that the required functions will be accessible from within the page.

```html
<html>
  <head><style>
      table.menu {font-family:Arial; font-size:9pt; width:80px;
        border-width:thin;border-style:outset;background-color:menu}
      td.menuitem {cursor:hand; background-color:menu}
  </style>
  <script language="JavaScript" src="jsfunctions.js"></script>
  </head>
  <body onclick="hideMenu('contextMenu');">
  <div id="contextMenu" style="position:absolute;display:none;">
    <table class="menu">
      <tr><td onclick="window.print();hideMenu('contextMenu');"
            onmouseover="this.style.backgroundColor='highlight';
                      this.style.color='highlighttext';"
            onmouseout="this.style.backgroundColor='menu';
                      this.style.color='menutext';"
          class="menuitem">Print</td></tr>
      <tr><td onclick="hideMenu('contextMenu');"
            onmouseover="this.style.backgroundColor='highlight';
                      this.style.color='highlighttext';"
          onmouseout="this.style.backgroundColor='menu';
                      this.style.color='menutext';"
          class="menuitem">Open</td></tr>
      <tr><td onclick="hideMenu('contextMenu');"
            onmouseover="this.style.backgroundColor='highlight';
                      this.style.color='highlighttext';"
          onmouseout="this.style.backgroundColor='menu';
                      this.style.color='menutext';"
          class="menuitem">Save</td></tr>
      <tr><td onclick="window.close();"
            onmouseover="this.style.backgroundColor='highlight';
                    this.style.color='highlighttext';"
            onmouseout="this.style.backgroundColor='menu';
                      this.style.color='menutext';"
          class="menuitem">Exit</td></tr>
    </table>
    </div>
    <a onmouseover="dispMenu('contextMenu');">Display menu</a>
    </body>
</html>
```

Figure 5.19: This code generates a custom "context menu."

The <body> element of the page has an onClick event that points
to the hideMenu() function for the menu. This will cause the
menu to disappear if the user clicks on an area of the screen
while the window is displayed. The <div> is defined with absolute positioning, and the "display" property is set to "none" to
keep the menu initially hidden. Then, a table is embedded within
the hidden <div>. The "class" attribute for this table is set to
"menu," which causes the style definition created in the internal
style sheet to be applied to this table.

The table contains four one-column rows. It is used to define the menu options themselves, along with the action to be performed if any one of the menu items is clicked. The style "class" for each <td> element is set to "menuitem," which causes that style to be applied to the menu options. The onmouseover and onmouseout events are defined to cause the menu option to be highlighted while the mouse cursor is over that option. To allow an event to fire when a user selects a menu option, an onClick event is defined for each <td> element.

The first option in the example, "Print," calls the window.print() method to cause the browser output to be sent to the printer. After that is done, this menu <div> is once again hidden, using the hideMenu() function. The "Open" and "Save" options work the same way, although they don't perform any actions in this simple example. Finally, the "Exit" option performs the window.close method to close the browser window. To control the display of this context menu, an <a> element is used with an onmouseover event that calls the dispMenu() function for the context menu.

Figure 5.20 shows what the output from this page looks like in the browser. When a user places the mouse over the Display menu link, the context menu is displayed automatically. When a user clicks on an option, the menu is hidden, and the action defined on the menu option's onClick event is fired.

The ability to use JavaScript to create a customized user interface within a browser application can be one of the most attractive arguments for making use of this language in a business environment. Another example of this type of functionality can be illustrated by using similar JavaScript coding techniques to create an application with what appears to be a "Windows Explorer" or "tree" type view.

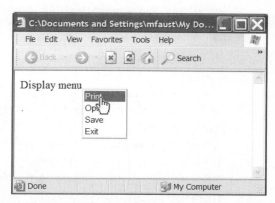

Figure 5.20: This is an example of a custom context menu.

This type of control allows users to navigate through any type of tree structure, such as files in a folder or individual pages within a web application. The expandFolder() function shown in Figure 5.21, which can be found in "jsfunctions.js," is used to accomplish this.

```
var closedFolder = new Image();
closedFolder.src = "folderc.gif";
var openFolder = new Image();
openFolder.src = "foldero.gif";

function expandFolder(brch, folder){

    var objBrch = document.getElementById(brch);

    if(objBrch.style.display == "none")
        objBrch.style.display = "block";
    else {
        objBrch.style.display = "none";}

    objFolder = document.getElementById(folder);
    if(objFolder.src.indexOf('folderc.gif')>-1)
        objFolder.src = openFolder.src;
    else
        objFolder.src = closedFolder.src;

}
```

Figure 5.21: This function is used to achieve a tree-view effect.

Note that the first portion of this example contains code that is located outside of the function itself. This code is executed within the page that loads "jsfunctions.js" and loads the required folder images into JavaScript objects. The function itself accepts two parameters. The first represents the ID associated with a <span> or <div> element containing the individual folder items. The second parameter represents the ID of the <div> that contains the folder icon and text.

The code toggles the "display" property for the element containing the items in the folder between "none" to hide the items and "block" to display them. Next, an object is created that is associated with the ID representing the folder image that corresponds to the folder <div>. Again, this code toggles between the opened and closed folder images.

The HTML code in Figure 5.22 illustrates how to use this function within a web page. Note that in this example, <div> elements represent folder-level objects and <span> elements contain the individual items within each folder. You could easily include an <a> element with each item, to create a hyperlink to that item.

```html
<html>
   <head>
      <title>JavaScript Tree Structure Example</title>
      <style>
        .folder{
      cursor: pointer;
      cursor: hand;
        }
      </style>
      <script language="JavaScript" src="jsfunctions.js"></script>
   </head>
   <body>
      <div class="folder" onClick="expandFolder('brch1', 'folder1');">
         <img src="folderc.gif" border="0" id="folder1">Folder 1
      </div>
        <span style="margin-left:36px; display:none" id="brch1">
        <img src="doc.gif">Item 1 <br>
        <img src="doc.gif">Item 2<br>
        <img src="doc.gif">Item 3<br>
      </span>
      <div class="folder" onClick="expandFolder('brch2', 'folder2');">
       <img src="folderc.gif" border="0" id="folder2">Folder 2
      </div>
        <span style="margin-left:36px; display:none"  id="brch2">
        <img src="doc.gif">Item 4 <br>
        <img src="doc.gif">Item 5<br>
        <div class="folder" onClick="expandFolder('brch3', 'folder3');">
         <img src="folderc.gif" border="0" id="folder3">Folder 3
        </div>
          <span style="margin-left:36px; display:none"  id="brch3">
             <img src="doc.gif">Item 6 <br>
           <img src="doc.gif">Item 7<br>
          </span>
      </span>
   </body>
</html>
```

Figure 5.22: This HTML page displays a tree structure.

Figure 5.23 shows what this example looks like in the browser. Note that we can create subfolders by embedding the same logic within the lower-level <span> element. JavaScript makes this functionality truly interactive, in that the expansion and contraction of the folder is done on the client browser, rather than having to submit data to the server and reload to display changes.

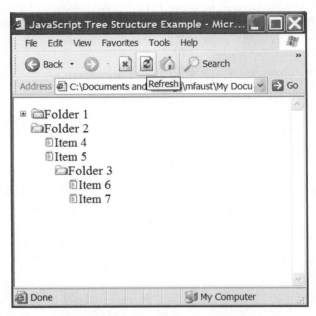

Figure 5.23: This sample tree structure is created using JavaScript.

Each of these examples helps illustrate exactly how you can use JavaScript functions to customize a simple web browser interface. It's easy to see that any of them can be extended and combined to create entirely new functionality.

Image Controls

Since browser-based applications give you the ability to display graphic image files, it's important to understand how to manipulate these image files. Fortunately, in JavaScript, you can do this fairly easily.

A common example of image-control is an image that changes when a mouse hovers over it. Figure 5.24 shows the source for the function switchImage(), which is found in "jsfunctions.js." This is an extremely simple function. It accepts a parameter that supplies the ID for the <img> element for which the function is being called, and a second parameter that supplies the source from which the new image should be loaded. The getElementById method associates the variable imgObj with the supplied <img> element. The "src" property changes the image to the one defined on the imgSrc variable.

```
function switchImage(imageID, imgSrc) {
    var imgObj = document.getElementById(imageID);
    imgObj.src = imgSrc;
}
```

Figure 5.24: This simple function switches from one image to another.

The HTML page shown in figure 5.25 illustrates how to use this function to switch images using the onmouseover/onmouseout events:

```
<html>
 <head>
  <script language="javaScript" src="jsfunctions.js"></script>
 </head>
 <body>
  <img id="image1" src="mouseoff.gif"
    onmouseover="switchImage('image1', 'mouseon.gif');"
    onmouseout="switchImage('image1', 'mouseoff.gif');">
 </body>
</html>
```

Figure 5.25: This example utilizes the switchImage() function.

This example creates a single <img> element with an ID of "image1." The source for this image is initially set to the file "mouseoff.gif." The onmouseover event calls the switchImage() function to switch the image to the image file "mouseon.gif." The onmouseout event returns the image back to the original "mouseoff.gif." It's important to note that the switchImage() function could have simply been written to use the "this" object to gain a reference to the object to be change. However, using the method of passing in an ID associated with the image gives the ability to use the function to change an image based on an event fired by another object, such as an input button.

Figure 5.26 illustrates the result of this example. As this example shows, the image is changed as the user places the mouse pointer over the object.

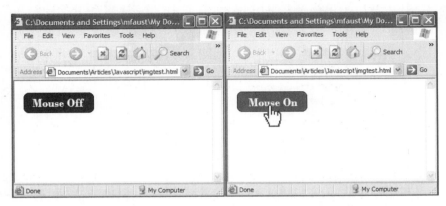

Figure 5.26: This example illustrates the use of the switchImage() function.

Image objects can be manipulated in other ways as well. It's actually possible to give a fade effect on an image displayed in the web browser. The fadeImg() function shown in Figure 5.27 is an example of how to do this.

```
function fadeImg(imageID, fadeAmt, fadeInOut) {
  var imgObj = document.getElementById(imageID);
  if (!fadeInOut) fadeInOUt = "IN";
  if (fadeInOut == "IN") {
    if (filterAmt <= 100) {
      imgObj.style.filter = "alpha(opacity:"+ filterAmt +")";
      imgObj.style.opacity = filterAmt;
      filterAmt += fadeAmt;
      var timeoutStr = "fadeImg('"+ imageID +"',"+ fadeAmt +",

              '" + fadeInOut + "')";
      window.setTimeout(timeoutStr, 100);
    }
    else window.clearTimeout();
  }
```

Figure 5.27: This function fades an image (part 1 of 2).

```
   if (fadeInOut == "OUT") {
     if (filterAmt >= 0) {
       imgObj.style.filter = "alpha(opacity:"+ filterAmt +")";
       imgObj.style.opacity = filterAmt;
       filterAmt -= fadeAmt;
       var timeoutStr = "fadeImg('"+imageID+"','"+fadeAmt+"',
                 '" + fadeInOut  +"')";
       window.setTimeout(timeoutStr, 100);
             }
         else window.clearTimeout();
  }
}
```

Figure 5.27: This function fades an image (part 2 of 2).

This function accepts three parameters. The first is a string that represents the ID for the <img> element to be faded. The second parameter identifies the speed at which the image should fade, using a value from one to 100, one being the slowest fade and 100 being an immediate fade. The third parameter for the fadeImg() function identifies whether the image should fade in or out, using a string value "IN" or "OUT."

This function uses two different methods of fading the image. The first is to use the "filter" style property. This property is supported by Internet Explorer to define an amount of opacity for the image. The second method uses the "opacity" style property, which is supported by Netscape's browser to perform the same function. The use of both of these helps provide maximum browser compatibility for the page. The amount of opacity is either increased or decreased by the amount provided on the fadeAmt variable each time the function is called. The setTimeout() function is then used to call the function every second, until the image has been completely faded in or out. Once that has happened, the clearTimeout() function is called to stop the calling of the function.

To see how to use the fadeImg() function, take a look at the sample HTML page in Figure 5.28. This example displays an image and allows a user to fade the displayed image out and back in by clicking a command button. When the image is displayed, the button can be used to fade the image out. Once it disappears, the button changes and can be used to fade the image back in.

```
<html>
 <head>
  <script language = "JavaScript" src="jsfunctions.js"></script>
  <script language = "JavaScript">

  function callFade() {
    var srcEl = window.event.srcElement;
    window.clearTimeout();
    if (srcEl.value == "Fade Out") {
        fadeImg("img1", 10, "OUT");
        srcEl.value = "Fade In";
        return;
    }
    if (srcEl.value == "Fade In") {
        fadeImg("img1", 10, "IN");
        srcEl.value = "Fade Out";
    }
  }
  </script>
 </head>
 <body>
  <img src = "mf.jpg" id="img1"><br>
  <br><input type="button" value="Fade Out"
onclick="callFade();">
 </body>
</html>
```

Figure 5.28: This page makes use of the fadeImg() function.

Images can also be used to create custom charts using JavaScript. Charts created with JavaScript can be dynamically changed without having to post data back to a web server. Simple bar charts can be created using the barChart() function/object shown in Figure 5.29.

```
function chartBar() {
    this.value=0;
    this.heading = "";
        }
function barChart(bars) {
    this.numberOfBars = bars;

    this.chartBars = new Array(bars);
    this.barColors = new Array(bars);
    for (x=0; x<this.numberOfBars; x++) {
        this.chartBars[x] = new chartBar();
        this.barColors[x] = "rgb(" + Math.floor(Math.random()*255)
```

Figure 5.29: This function can be used to create simple bar charts using JavaScript (part 1 of 2).

```
                          + ", "+ Math.floor(Math.random()*255) + ", "
                          + Math.floor(Math.random()*255) + ")";
        }
        this.chartTitle = "";
        this.chartWidth = 0;

        this.showChart = function() {
        var min = 9999999999;
        var max = 0;
        // Determine MIN and MAX chart values
        for (x=0; x<this.numberOfBars; x++) {
          if (this.chartBars[x].value > max) {
             max = this.chartBars[x].value;
          }
          if (this.chartBars[x].value < min) {
             min = this.chartBars[x].value;
          }
        }

        document.write("<table cellspacing=0 width=" + this.chartWidth + ">");
        document.write("<tr><td align=center colspan =
          "+this.numberOfBars+">"+this.chartTitle+"</td></tr>");
        document.write("<tr><td>");
        document.write("<table height=95% style='border-right:
          thin solid black;'>");
        var incr = Math.round((max - min) / 10);
        var chartIndex = max;
        for (x = 0; x <10; x++) {
           document.write("<tr height=10%><td height=100% align='Right'>"
             + chartIndex + "</td></tr>");
           chartIndex -= incr;
        }
        document.write("</table></td>");

        for (x=0; x<this.numberOfBars; x++) {
             var barWidth = (this.chartWidth/this.numberOfBars) - 20;
             var barHeight = (this.chartBars[x].value / (max-min))
               * (this.chartHeight-50);
             document.write("<td valign='bottom' style='border-bottom:
               thin solid black;' width=100>");
             document.write("<table valign=top style='border:
               thin solid black;background-color:" + this.barColors[x]
               + ";width:"+ barWidth + ";height:" + barHeight
               + "'><tR><td></td></tr></table></td>");
        }
        document.write("</tr><tr><td></td>");
        for (x=0; x<this.numberOfBars; x++) {
             document.write("<td valign='Middle'
style='writing-mode:tb-rl;filter: flipH() flipV();'>" +
this.chartBars[x].heading + "</td>");
        }

        document.write("</tr></table>");

            }
}
```

Figure 5.29: This function can be used to create simple bar charts using JavaScript (part 2 of 2).

Notice that there are actually two objects defined here. The barChart() object depends on a chartBar() object, which is used to define individual bars within the chart. The chartBar() object supports a "value" property to define the value for the bar and a "heading" property to define the text displayed beneath the bar.

The barChart() object itself is created with a single parameter that identifies the number of bars to be displayed in the chart. The chartBars property is created as an array of chartBar() objects. A barColors array is also created to allow you to define the colors of the individual bars in the chart. These values can be provided when the object is used; otherwise, random colors will be displayed.

A chartTitle property is supported to display a heading at the top of the chart. The properties chartWidth and chartHeight are both available to define the width and height of the chart. A showChart() method is built into the object to cause the actual displaying of the chart in our page. This method calculates minimum and maximum values for the chart. These values are used to generate the numeric values along the side of the chart.

The chart itself is created as an HTML table. Each of the bars is generated using the value provided. Next, the heading for each bar is displayed along the bottom of the chart area. Note that special CSS properties cause this text to be rotated 90 degrees. The HTML page in Figure 5.30 illustrates the use of the barChart() function.

```
<html>
 <head>
  <script language="JavaScript" src="jsfunctions.js"></script>
 </head>
 <body>
  <script language="JavaScript">
   var cht1 = new barChart(12);

   cht1.chartTitle = "Annual Sales Chart";
   cht1.chartWidth = 800;
   cht1.chartHeight = 300;
   cht1.chartBars[0].value = 10000;
   cht1.chartBars[1].value = 12750;
   cht1.chartBars[2].value = 20500;
   cht1.chartBars[3].value = 44000;
   cht1.chartBars[4].value = 20075;
   cht1.chartBars[5].value = 50875;
   cht1.chartBars[6].value = 40075;
   cht1.chartBars[7].value = 27500;
   cht1.chartBars[8].value = 17500;
   cht1.chartBars[9].value = 65955;
   cht1.chartBars[10].value = 78750;
   cht1.chartBars[11].value = 63200;

   cht1.chartBars[0].heading = "January";
   cht1.chartBars[1].heading = "February";
   cht1.chartBars[2].heading = "March";
   cht1.chartBars[3].heading = "April";
   cht1.chartBars[4].heading = "May";
   cht1.chartBars[5].heading = "June";
   cht1.chartBars[6].heading = "July";
   cht1.chartBars[7].heading = "August";
   cht1.chartBars[8].heading = "September";
   cht1.chartBars[9].heading = "October";
   cht1.chartBars[10].heading = "November";
   cht1.chartBars[11].heading = "December";

   cht1.showChart();
  </script>
 </body>
</html>
```

Figure 5.30: This page uses the barChart() object to display a chart.

This example first creates a reference to the barChart() object for
the variable "cht1" to create a bar chart with 12 bars. Next, the
"width" and "height" properties are defined, as well as the individual values for each bar in the chart and their headings (representing the 12 months of the year). Finally, the showChart()

method is called to cause the newly defined chart to be displayed, as shown in Figure 5.31.

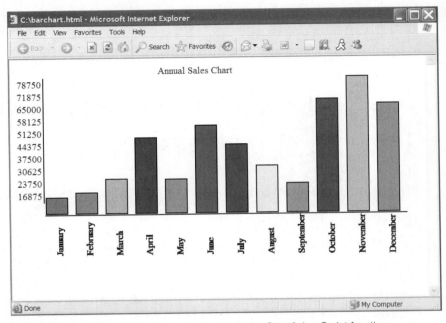

Figure 5.31: This example was created using the barChart() JavaScript function.

As you can see, a relatively small amount of JavaScript code can easily generate this chart. This example helps to further illustrate the power of user-defined functions within JavaScript applications.

Summary

As with other programming languages, JavaScript enables you to encapsulate commonly used tasks into functions that can be utilized in different situations as needed. This modular design helps to extend the usability of JavaScript for building efficient business applications. You've seen a few examples here of usable functions that you can incorporate into your browser-based applications. The real power comes when you create your own JavaScript.

CHAPTER 6

Asynchronous JavaScript and XML

One of the few shortcomings of JavaScript is its lack of support for standardized data-access APIs like ODBC or JDBC. Fortunately, there is an alternate means for giving a client-side JavaScript routine access to server data. *Asynchronous JavaScript and XML*, or *AJAX*, gives you the ability to read data from a variety of sources. This data can be XML data, HTML data, or even a simple text file. This truly powerful capability further extends the usability of JavaScript as a mainstream development language for business programmers. In this chapter, you'll explore what AJAX is and how to use it to read server data into a JavaScript routine.

AJAX: It's Not Just for Cleaning Anymore

Pardon the pun, but I thought we needed to get that one out of the way right away. The technology behind AJAX has actually been around for several years. This technology was developed by Microsoft and was initially known as *remote scripting*. The key component that makes AJAX possible is the XMLHttpRequest object, which is currently supported by all modern web browsers. Microsoft Outlook Web Access, a popular solution for accessing business e-mail remotely, is an example of an application built using the XMLHttpRequest object. AJAX is also the key to dynamic web sites such as Google's G-Mail and Google Maps.

AJAX allows you to create programs with a user interface that is more like a standalone application than a browser-based application. This is because the JavaScript application is able to send data to and receive data from a server without have to reload the entire page.

The method you use to define an XMLHttpRequest object depends on which browser you are using. The first example below illustrates the method used in Internet Explorer, while the second illustrates the method supported by Mozilla and other browsers:

```
// Internet Explorer Method
var objXML = new ActiveXObject("Microsoft.XMLHTTP");

// Mozilla, Netscape, etc…
var objXML1 = new XMLHttpRequest();
```

The first method makes use of the ActiveXObject to create a reference to the Microsoft.XMLHTTP ActiveX control. The second method simply creates a new instance of the XMLHttpRequest object itself. Once this object has been defined, your client script has a set of properties and methods that can be used to retrieve data from a defined server. Table 6.1 lists the properties supported by the XMLHttpRequest object.

Table 6.1: Properties Supported by the XMLHttpRequest Object	
Property	**Description**
onreadystatechange	This event handler is launched each time the ready state changes.
readyState	This is the ready state of the request.
responseText	This is the server response as a text string.
responseXML	This is the server response in an XML document.
status	This is the HTTP numeric status ("404" = not found, for example).
statusText	This is the HTTP status as a text string ("Not Found," for example).

The onreadystatechange property defines a function to be called when the value of the readyState property changes. The readyState property returns a value identifying the state of the XML request. Values returned are shown below:

- 0 = uninitialized
- 1 = loading
- 2 = loaded
- 3 = interactive
- 4 = complete

The responseText property reads the response from the server as a text string. The responseXML property also reads the server response, but returns the data into an XML document object. The status property retrieves the numeric status of the XML request. Common codes returned by this property include 404 to indicate a document is not found, or 200 for an "OK" status. The text associated with the status property can be retrieved via the statusText property. In addition to these properties, the XMLHttpRequest object also supports a set of methods, shown in Table 6.2.

Table 6.2: Methods Supported by the XMLHttpRequest Object	
Method	**Description**
abort()	This method aborts the current XML request.
getAllResponseHeaders()	This method returns the HTTP headers associated with the request.
getResponseHeader()	This method returns a value for the HTTP header specified on the defined parameter.
open()	This method defines parameters associated with an XML request, including the URL and method.
send()	This method sends the XML request to the server.
setRequestHeader()	This method defines the request header values for the XML request.

The open() method lets you define information related to the server and the document from which the data is being retrieved. The parameters supplied on this method are shown here:

```
open(method, URL, asnyc)
```

The "method" value identifies the method used to communicate with the server: "GET" for retrieving data from the server, or "POST" for sending data to the server. The "URL" value supplies the Uniform Resource Locator of the document to be read. "Asnyc" is a true/false value that identifies whether or not the connection is to be made asynchronously. If the connection is made asynchronously, the script continues execution without waiting for results from the server. If the "ansyc" value is false, the script will wait for a response from the server before continuing execution. Because many factors come into play when connecting to a remote system, it's not always the best idea to make asynchronous connections. If, for example, a server is down or unreachable, you wouldn't want your script to hang indefinitely.

The open() method defines the connection to the server, but the actual connection is not initiated until the send() method is executed. The optional parameter for this method supplies data to be posted to the server as a string. As mentioned earlier, when a connection is made asynchronously, the script continues execution immediately after this statement is executed. Otherwise, the script will wait for a response from the server before continuing.

Here is an example of the code required to make a connection using the open() and send()methods and the XMLHttpRequest object:

```
var parms  = encodeURI(
        "parm1=" + value1 + ";parm2=" + value2);

var requestXML = new XMLHttpRequest();

requestXML.open("POST", "http://some.webserver.com/XMLdata");
requestXML.send(parms);
```

In this example, the variable "parms" is created to contain data to be posted to the server. The XMLHttpRequest object is then defined and used with open() to connect to the defined web server using the "POST" method. The send() method opens the connection using the "parms" defined in the first part of the script.

The setRequestHeader() method identifies HTTP header values. The two string parameters supplied to this method represent the HTTP header name and the value to be supplied for that header. The example below illustrates the use of this method to define the HTTP header "Content-Type" value:

```
req.sendRequestHeader('Content-Type', 'application/vnd.ms-excel');
```

Note that the first parameter identifies the header name, while the second parameter identifies the new value for the header. This example indicates that the MIME content type for the document being accessed is Microsoft Excel.

These basic properties and methods of the XMLHttpRequest object give you the ability to retrieve an enormous amount of information from readily available web services. To examine just how powerful this capability is, let's take a look at an example that consumes web services.

AJAX, Step by Step

To make a connection to a remote document using the XMLHttpRequest object, a simple series of steps needs to be followed. The first step is to define the XMLHttpRequest object itself. Your script needs to allow for the fact that Internet Explorer uses a different method of defining this object than other browsers. The statements below show how to do this:

```
if (!ActiveXObject) {
    xmlHttp = new XMLHttpRequest;
  }
else {
    xmlHttp = new ActiveXObject("Microsoft.XMLHTTP");
  }
```

This example checks for the existence of the ActiveXObject object. If that object does not exist, it's assumed that the document is being displayed on a browser other than Internet Explorer. In that case, the object is defined using the XMLHttpRequest object. Otherwise, it is defined using the ActiveXObject("Microsoft.XMLHTTP") object.

Now that the object has been defined, the next steps are to identify how to use this object to connect to the target document, and then make the actual connection. The lines below illustrates how to accomplish this:

```
xmlHttp.open("GET","http://some.webservice.site/document.xml", true);
xmlHttp.send();
```

As this example shows, you first use the open() method to define information about the document you're requesting. Here, the first value ("GET") defines the method used to connect to the web server whose URL is the next value. The final value indicates that this connection should be made asynchronously, which means that once the send() method is executed, execution of the script will continue without waiting for data being returned. The send() method sends the request defined on the open() method.

Once the connection has been made, you need to associate a JavaScript function with the onreadystatechange event. This function can be either an embedded function or a user-defined function name. Here are examples of both methods:

```
// Defining event handler using a user-defined function
   xmlHttp.onreadystatechange = stateHandler(xmlHttp);

// Defining the event handler using an internal function definition
   xmlHttp.onreadystatechange = function(xmlHttp) {
      alert(xmlHttp.readyState);
   }
```

The first example is fairly simple. It just assigns the onreadystatechange event to the stateHandler() function. The second example uses a technique whereby the function itself is embedded into the assignment statement. Note that the xmlHttp object is passed as a parameter to each function. Since the onreadystatechange() function is called each time the ready state changes, the application needs to ensure that the code to be performed is only executed if and when the proper state is reached.

This can be done by conditioning the code to be executed, as shown below:

```
if (xmlHttp.readyState ==4) {
   if (xmlHttp.status == 200) {
   // Code to be executed once an XML document is openened.
   }
   }
```

This example compares the readyState to 4, which indicates the connection has been made. It also compares the returned "status" value to 200, which is the "OK" status from the server, indicating the connection is open.

Once you have a successful connection, you need a way to get the data returned. The first step in this process is to assign a variable to the responseXML property on the XMLHttpRequest object, as shown here:

```
var xmldoc = xmlHttp.responseXML;
```

When that association has been built, the variable xmldoc automatically becomes a type XMLDocument. This type lets you traverse the entire structure of the returned document. Next, the getElementsByTagName() method gives you access to individual elements within the returned document, based on their tag names. This method returns a collection of elements that you can read using the item() collection. To read the actual data stored in the element, use the firstChild.data property. Here is an example of reading through each element of the collection and writing out the results:

```
var myData = xmldoc.getElementsByTagName("datatag");

for (var x = 0; x < myData.length; x++) {
   document.write(myData.item(x).firstChild.data);
   }
```

This example assigns the variable myData to the collection associated with the XML tag named "data." The "length" property determines the upper boundary for a "for" loop to read through all of the items in this collection. The code then uses the firstChild.data property to display the values out to the browser. You can also traverse the tree structure using the childNodes collection, as described in chapter 2.

This simple process gives you all the tools you need to access XML data via AJAX. Now, let's take a look at a working example of using AJAX.

An XML Weather Tool

The simple JavaScript application shown in Figure 6.1 gives you a great start at using AJAX to retrieve data from a remote server. It allows you to display a seven-day forecast from the National Weather Service in your browser, strictly using JavaScript and XML.

```
<html>
<head>
<title>XML Weather Tool</title>
<script language="JavaScript">
    var weatherXMLDoc, weatherXMLObj, xmlHttpNWS, xmlHttpZip,  dataTable
    var cityName, myIcons, myTime, myTemp, fcstDate, fullDate
    var dow =["Sunday","Monday","Tuesday","Wednesday","Thursday",
              "Friday","Saturday","Sunday"]

    if (!ActiveXObject) {
       xmlHttpNWS = new XMLHttpRequest;
       xmlHttpZip = new XMLHttpRequest;
     }
    else {
      xmlHttpZip = new ActiveXObject("Microsoft.XMLHTTP");
      xmlHttpNWS = new ActiveXObject("Microsoft.XMLHTTP");
     }

function getNWSForecast() {
    var zipCode = document.all("zipcode").value;


xmlHttpZip.open("GET","http://api.local.yahoo.com/MapsService/V1/geocode?" +
                 "appid=YahooDemo&zip=" + zipCode, false);
    xmlHttpZip.send();

    var zipXMLDoc = xmlHttpZip.responseXML;
    var
lat=zipXMLDoc.getElementsByTagName("Latitude").item(0).firstChild.data;
    var
lon=zipXMLDoc.getElementsByTagName("Longitude").item(0).firstChild.data;
```

Figure 6.1: This page generates a seven-day forecast using JavaScript (part 1 of 3).

```
    cityName = zipXMLDoc.getElementsByTagName("City").item(0).firstChild.data
+
        "," +
zipXMLDoc.getElementsByTagName("State").item(0).firstChild.data;
    var requestURL = "http://www.weather.gov/forecasts/xml/SOAP_server/" +
                    "ndfdXMLclient.php?lat=" + lat + "&lon=" + lon +
                "&product=time-series&begin=2004-01-01T00%3A00%3A00&" +

"end=2010-07-11T00%3A00%3A00&temp=temp&icons=icons&Submit=Submit";

    xmlHttpNWS.open("GET", requestURL , true);
    xmlHttpNWS.send();
    xmlHttpNWS.onreadystatechange = displayNWSForecast;
}

function displayNWSForecast() {
    dataTable = document.all("myTable");
    var tableCaption = dataTable.createCaption();
    tableCaption.innerHTML = "NWS Forecast for " + cityName;
    var col = 0;

    var weatherXMLDoc = xmlHttpNWS.responseXML;
    myIcons=weatherXMLDoc.getElementsByTagName("icon-link");
    myTime=weatherXMLDoc.getElementsByTagName("start-valid-time");
    myTemp=weatherXMLDoc.getElementsByTagName("value");
    var loopQty = myIcons.length;

    for(var x=0; x < loopQty; x++) {

      fcstDate = new Date(eval('"' +
              myTime.item(x).firstChild.data.substring(5,7) + "/" +
              myTime.item(x).firstChild.data.substring(8,10) +"/" +
              myTime.item(x).firstChild.data.substring(0,4) +'"'));
      fullDate = new Date(eval('"' +
              myTime.item(x).firstChild.data.substring(5,7) +"/" +
              myTime.item(x).firstChild.data.substring(8,10) +"/" +
              myTime.item(x).firstChild.data.substring(0,4) + " " +
              myTime.item(x).firstChild.data.substring(11,19) + '"'));

      if (fullDate.getHours() >= 12 && fullDate.getHours() <=14) {
        myTable.rows[0].cells[col + 1].innerHTML = dow[fcstDate.getDay()];
        myTable.rows[0].cells[col + 1].align = "center";
        myTable.rows[0].cells[col + 1].style.backgroundColor = "Red";
        myTable.rows[0].cells[col + 1].style.color = "White";
        myTable.rows[1].cells[col + 1].innerHTML = "<img src='" +
                myIcons.item(x).firstChild.data + "'><br>" +
                myTemp.item(x).firstChild.data;
        myTable.rows[1].cells[col + 1].align = "center";
        myTable.rows[0].cells[col + 1].innerHTML = dow[fcstDate.getDay()];
        myTable.rows[0].cells[col + 1].style.backgroundColor = "Red";
        myTable.rows[0].cells[col + 1].style.color = "White";
        if (col > 6) {
        x = loopQty;}
```

Figure 6.1: This page generates a seven-day forecast using JavaScript (part 2 of 3).

```
          else col = col + 1;

      }
  ;
    }
  }
}

</script>
</head>
<body><p align="CENTER">
<input type="text" name="zipcode" maxlength=10 style="width:75px">
<input  type="button" value="Get Forecast" onClick="getNWSForecast();">
<table id="myTable" border=0 cellpadding=1 cellspacing=3>

      </TD>    </TD>    </TD>    </TD>    </TD>    </TD>    </TD>    </TD></TR>

      </TD>    </TD>    </TD>    </TD>    </TD>    </TD>    </TD>    </TD></TR>
</table>
</p>
</body>
</html>
```

Figure 6.1: This page generates a seven-day forecast using JavaScript (part 3 of 3).

The functionality of this example was introduced in chapter 1. As mentioned in that chapter, this example actually consumes two different web services. The first is a Yahoo.com mapping service that can be used to obtain the longitude and latitude for a given U. S. zip code. The second web service, from the National Weather Service, can be used to retrieve detailed weather-forecast data for a location based on its longitude and latitude. The initial XMLHttpRequest objects for each of the web services are defined outside of any function. The routine checks for the existence of the ActiveXObject object to determine if the page is being displayed on an Internet Explorer browser. This is done to help decide exactly how to define the XMLHttpRequest object.

The HTML portion of this page defines a text input box, a command button, and an HTML table with two rows and seven columns. This will be populated later with the forecast data. The command button is used to trigger the getNWSForecast() function. The xmlHttpZip object is defined to be opened using the "GET" method, along with the URL associated with the map-data web service. This XMLHttpRequest object is defined as a synchronous request because of the relatively small amount of data to be retrieved. The variable zipXMLDoc is associated with the XML response using the responseXML property of the xmlHttpZip object. This association supplies the XML data in a parsed format that allows individual tags to be read using the getElementByTagName method. Because of the nature of this request, only a single value is returned. This value is accessed through the item(0).firstChild.data property. At this point, the code has retrieved the longitude, latitude, city, and state abbreviation associated with the supplied zip code.

The longitude and latitude values are used to build the URL associated with the National Weather Service web service. The object xmlHttpNWS is created as an XMLHttpRequest. This URL defines the specific pieces of information being requested from the web service. This time, the request is processed asynchronously because of the amount of time that can elapse between when the request is made and when the web service returns the data to the client. Associating the displayNWSForecast() object with the onreadystatechange event handler allow the data to be processed when it is returned. This event is fired when the ready-state value changes for the XMLHttpRequest object.

Within the displayNWSForecast() function, a JavaScript variable is associated with the HTML table that is built within the HTML section of the page. Remember that this function is called whenever the ready-state value changes. Because of this, you need to ensure that the ready state has reached a value of 4, or "complete," before attempting to read data from the response. The weatherXMLDoc variable is associated with the responseXML property of the xmlHttpNWS object. This gives access to all of the child nodes of the returned XML document.

As mentioned earlier, the code only requests specific pieces of information related to the weather forecast. In this case, it requests the numeric value that identifies the temperature forecast and the URL for an image file that acts as a graphic representation of the weather forecast. The forecast data is returned automatically. To access each of these node lists, a JavaScript variable is associated with each one, once again using the getElementsByTagName() property. Once these associations are created, the data from the collections can be read.

The forecast data provided by the NWS is returned at four-hour intervals. We want to only display the forecast data for whatever update occurs between 12 P.M. and 2 P.M. The individual nodes are read using the item(x).firstChild.data property, where x indicates an index value identifying which node in the list to access. The retrieved values are used to populate the HTML table described earlier. Once seven days have been displayed, the application exits the "for" loop.

Note that the value retrieved from the myIcons collection is a URL that points to the location of an image file representing the forecast for the displayed day. This value is supplied as the "src" attribute on an <img> element, causing the forecast icon to be displayed within the resulting seven-day forecast.

Figure 6.2 shows a sample Web page resulting from the code in Figure 6.1. Remember that this example reads XML data and changes the contents of the web page, all without having to post the entire page back to the server. This simple, yet powerful, example illustrates exactly how easy it is to retrieve and use data from a web service with JavaScript and AJAX.

The number of readily available web services continues to grow every day. You can freely retrieve information via public web services from companies like Federal Express, UPS, Amazon, Yahoo, and Google, just to name a few. In addition, government web services allow you to get weather forecasts from the National Weather Service, get currency exchange rates from the Federal Reserve Bank, or even process transactions with the U. S. Postal Service. AJAX and XML web services make JavaScript an even more powerful tool for business programmers.

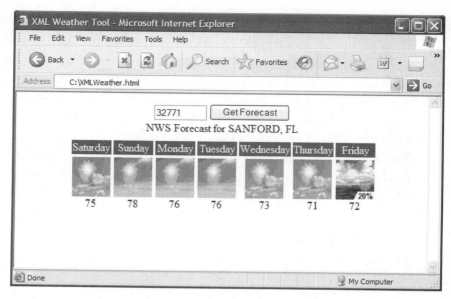

Figure 6. 2: The output from the XML weather-tool AJAX example.

The Wide World of the Web

Yet another amazing aspect of JavaScript is the amount of code that is freely available on the Internet. There's almost no task you could want to perform for which you can't find sample JavaScript code. Much of that code is freely redistributable at no cost to the developer. Table 6.3 lists just a few of the valuable resources for sample JavaScript code.

Table 6.3: Useful Resources for JavaScript Programming Information	
Website URL	**Description**
http://java.sun.com/javascript/	Sun's JavaScript educational web site
http://www.mozilla.org/js/scripting/	JavaScript information from Mozilla
http://www.w3schools.com/js/	JavaScript educational resources from w3Schools.com
http://javascript.internet.com/	The JavaScript Source web site
http://msdn2.microsoft.com/en-us/library/yek4tbz0.aspx	Microsoft's Jscript Users' Guide web site

Summary

Whether you're looking to dynamically change the look of your web page, validate form data, or even access remote servers using AJAX, the business case for JavaScript has never been stronger. Hopefully, the techniques you've learned in this book will help lead you down the path toward building dynamic browser-based business applications with JavaScript.

Appendix

Javascript Language Quick Reference

The tables in this appendix are intended as a quick reference to JavaScript language elements and CSS properties.

JavaScript Elements

The tables in this section contain JavaScript language elements, including operators and special characters, along with the properties and methods associated with the "document" and "window" objects.

Table A.1: JavaScript Special Characters	
Control Character	**Description**
\f	Form-feed
\r	Carriage return
\n	Linefeed
\t	Horizontal tab.
\v	Vertical tab.
\0	Annual character.
\b	Backspace.
\s	Whitespace (any of [\f\n\r\t\v\u00A0\u2028\u2029]).
\S	Not whitespace
\w	Any alphanumerical character.
\W	Any non-word characters
\d	Any digit
\D	Any non-digit
\xxx	Character with the 2 digit hex code xx
\uxxxx	Unicode character with the four digit hex code xxxx

Operator	Type	Description
Table A.2: JavaScript Variable Operators		
Operator	**Type**	**Description**
+	Numeric	Addition (result = value1 + value2)
-	Numeric	Subtraction (result = value1 - value2)
*	Numeric	Multiplication (result = value1 * value2)
/	Numeric	Division (result = value1 / value2)
%	Numeric	Modulus – remainder after division(result = value1 % value2)
++	Numeric (Unary)	Increment by 1 (result++)
—	Numeric (Unary)	Decrement by 1 (result—)
+	String	Concatenate (stringreslut = string1 + string2)
==	Comparison	Equal to (value1 == value2)
!=	Comparison	Is Not Equal to (value1 != value2)
>	Comparison	Greater than (value1 > value2)
>=	Comparison	Greater than or Equal to (value1 >= value2)
<	Comparison	Less than (value1 < value2)
<=	Comparison	Less than or Equal to (value1 <= value2)
===	Comparison	Identical — Equal to with type comparison (value1 === value2)
!==	Comparison	Not Identical (value1 !== value2)
=	Assignment	Set value (result = value)
+=	Assignment	Increment and set (result += 12 would be the same as result = result + 12)
-=	Assignment	Decrement and set (result -= 12)
*=	Assignment	Multiply and set (result *= 2)
/=	Assignment	Divide and set (result /= 3)
%=	Assignment	Perform modulus and set (result %= 6)
&=	Assignment	Perform Bitwise AND and set value (result &= value)
|=	Assignment	Perform Bitwise OR and set value (result |= value)
^=	Assignment	Perform Bitwise XOR and set value (result |= value)

Table A.2: JavaScript Variable Operators		
Operator	**Type**	**Description**
<<=	Assignment	Bitwise Left shift and set with 0 fill (result <<= 2)
>>=	Assignment	Bitwise Right shift and set self-propagating (Result >>= 2)
>>>=	Assignment	Bitwise Right shift and set with 0 fill (result >>>= 2)
&&	Boolean	Logical AND operation if(val1=1 && val2=2)
||	Boolean	Logical OR operation if(val1=1 || val2=2)
!	Boolean	Logical NOT operation (if !(val1 = val2))
&	Bitwise	Bitwise AND (result = val1 & val2
|	Bitwise	Bitwise OR (result = val1 & val2)
~	Bitwise	Bitwise NOT (result =!bit1)
<<	Bitwise	Bitwise Left Shift/zero fill (result = 8 << 2)
>>	Bitwise	Bitwise Right Shift/self-propagating (result = 8 >> 2)
>>>	Bitwise	Bitwise Right Shift/zero fill (result = 8 >>> 2)

Table A.3: JavaScript Bitwise Operators	
Statement	**Operation description**
X = 7 & 43;	00000111 & 00101011 = 00000011 = 3
X= 7 | 43	00000111 | 00101011 = 00101111 = 47
X= ^7	~ 0111 = -1000 = -8
<<	0000 0100 << 4 = 0100 0000 or 4 << 4 = 64
>>	0000 1100 >> 2 = 0000 0011 or 12 >> 2 = 3
>>>	0000 1100 >>> 2 = 0000 0011 or 12 >>> 2 = 3

Table A.4: Properties Associated with the "window" Object

Property	Description
window.closed	This property returns a Boolean value that identifies whether or not a specific window has been closed.
window.defaultStatus	Used to access the information displayed in the status bar once the document loads.
window.dialogArguments	Used to retrieve variables passed into a browser dialog window.
window.dialogHeight	Reads and updates the height of a browser dialog window.
window.dialogLeft	Reads and updates the leftmost coordinate of a browser dialog window.
window.dialogTop	Reads and updates the top coordinate of a browser dialog window
window.dialogWidth	Reads and updates the width of a browser dialog window.
window.length	Identifies the number of frames within the window object.
window.name	Used to set or read the name of the window object.
window.offscreenBuffering	A Boolean value that identifies whether or not the window is generated off screen prior to displaying to the user.
window.opener	Used as a reference to the window that opened the current window.
window.parent	Identifies the parent of the current window.
window.returnValue	Used to define a return value from a browser dialog window to the main browser window.
window.screenLeft	The leftmost position of the browser window relative to the screen
window.screenTop	The top position of the browser window relative to the screen.
window.self	Used to reference the current window.
window.status	Used to read or update the status bar text for the browser window.
window.top	Used to identify the uppermost parent window to the current window.

Table A.5: Event Handlers Associated with the "window" Object

Event	Description
window.onblur	Defines action to be performed when the window is no longer in focus.
window.onerror	Defines action to be performed when the an error event occurs within the browser window,
window.onfocus	Defines the action to perform when the window gains focus..
window.onload	Defines the action to perform when the window initially loads.
window.onresize	Defines the action to be performed when the window is resized.
window.onunload	Defines an action to perform when the window "unloads" prior to closing.

Table A.6: Methods Used to Perform Actions on a Browser Window

Method	Description
window.alert()	Displays a simple dialog box with a specified message. This dialog only displays an OK button.
window.blur()	Takes focus away from the current window.
window.clearInterval()	Clears a timeout set using setInterval().
window.clearTimeout()	Clears a timeout set using setTimeout().
window.close()	Closes the window.
window.confirm()	Displays a simple dialog box with a specified message. This dialog displays OK and a Cancel buttons.
window.createPopup()	Creates a new pop-up window.
window.focus()	Puts the window in focus.
window.moveBy(x,y)	Moves the window by a specified number of pixels.
window.moveTo(*left,top*)	Moves the window to the location identified by the left and top values.
window.navigate(*url location*)	Navigates to the URL supplied.
window.open()	Opens a new browser window.
window.print()	Sends the contents of the browser window to the printer.
window.prompt()	Displays a dialog box that prompts the user to enter a response.

Table A.6: Methods Used to Perform Actions on a Browser Window

Method	Description
window.resizeBy()	Resizes the window by a specified number of pixels.
window.resizeTo()	Resizes the window to a specific width and height.
window.scrollBy()	Scrolls the content by the specified number of pixels.
window.scrollTo()	Scrolls the content to the specified coordinates.
window.setInterval(*action, window.interval*)	Performs a specified task every time the number of milliseconds specified on the interval parameter has passed.
window.setTimeout()	Performs a specified task after the provided number of milliseconds has passed.
window.showModalDialog (*url,options*)	Displays the supplied URL in a Modal Dialog box.
window.showModelessDialog(*url, options*)	Displays the supplied URL in a Modeless Dialog box.

Table A.7: Options Used with the "window.open" Method

Option	Values	Description
fullscreen	yes/no	Identifies whether or not to display the window in fullscreen mode.
height	number	Used to define the height in pixels of the window.
left	number	Used to define the leftmost corner in pixels for the left side of window.
location	yes/no	Used to define whether or not to display the location bar containing the page URL.
menubar	yes/no	Identifies whether or not to display the browser's menu bar.
resizable	yes/no	Used to define whether or not the window should be resizable.
scrollbars	yes/no	Used to control whether or not scroll bars are displayed.
status	yes/no	Identifies whether or not the status bar should be displayed.
titlebar	yes/no	Identifies whether or not the title bar should be displayed.
toolbar	yes/no	Identifies whether or not the toolbar should be displayed.
top	number	Used to define the upper corner position of the top of the browser window in pixels.
width	number	Used to define the width in pixels of the browser window.

Table A.8: Objects Implemented within the "window" Object

Object	Description
window.document	This object is used to access the document displayed within the browser.
window.event	Used to access information about events occurring within the browser.
window.history	This object can be used to access URLs that the user accessed from within the parent browser window.
window.location	This object contains the current URL for the document displayed in the current window.
window.navigation	This object is used to access data related to the user's browser client.
window.screen	This object is used to access data related to the user's display screen.

Table A.9: Properties Associated with the "document" Object

Property	Description
document.alinkColor	Identifies the color of an active link within the document.
document.bgColor	Used to read or set the background color for the document.
document.body	Defines the document body.
cookie	Used to access cookies associated with the document.
document.domain	Gets the server domain name for the document.
document.fgColor	Used to read or set the foreground color for the document.
document.lastModified	Returns a value indicating the data and time the document was last modified.
document.linkColor	Reads and sets the color to be used for links within the document.
document.referrer	Gets a value identifying the document that referred to the current document.
document.title	Retrieves the title for the document.
document.URL	Retrieves the URL for the document.
document.vlinkColor	Reads and sets the color for links in the document that were previously visited.

Table A.10: Collections Implemented within the "document" Object

Collection	Description
document.anchors	This collection contains all of the anchor (<a>) elements with a defined name.
document.applets	Used to access all of the applet objects (<object>) tags within the document body.
document.forms	Gives access to all of the <form> objects within the document body, and all of the elements within those forms.
document.images	This collection contains all of the images (<img> tag) within the document body.
document.links	This collection is used to access all of the HTML hyperlink elements (14).

Table A.11: Methods to Perform Actions on the "document" Object

Method	Description
document.clear()	Removes all child elements in the document.
document.close()	Closes an output data stream and displays the resulting data.
document.createAttribute(*attrName*)	Creates a new attribute.
document.createElement(*html tag*)	Creates a new child document element.
document.createTextNode(*text string*)	Creates a simple text string.
document.focus()	Places the document in focus.
document.getElementById(*id*)	Allows access to specific document elements based on the elements ID attribute.
document.getElementsByName(*name*)	Gives access to a collection of specific document elements based on the "name" attribute.
document.getElementsByTagName(*tag name*)	Accesses a collection of elements based the tag name.
document.open()	Opens a document for writing.
document.write(*string*)	Writes a string of text to the document.
document.writeln(*string*)	Writes a string of text to the document followed by a line feed. Used with *document.op en()*.

CSS Properties

The following tables provide a concise reference for cascading style sheet elements.

Table A.12: CSS Object Properties	
Property	**Description**
background	This property can be used to define any of the other background properties.
background-attachment	This property identifies whether a defined background image is fixed or scrolls with the rest of the window. Possible values are "scroll" and "fixed." This property is used when the background-image is also specified.
background-color	The background color for the document is defined using this property. The value can be defined as a color name, an RGB value, or a hex color code.
background-image	This is used to define an image file to be displayed as the background for a defined HTML document.
background-position	The position of a background image within the document is defined using this property. This value can be specified as a constant (top left, etc..), a % of the page down and across from the top left corner (10% 25%), or a specific number of pixles down and across from the top left corner.
background-repeat	This value identifies whether or not a background image should be repeated throughout the document.
border	Allows us to set all border properties in a single declaration.
border-bottom	Used to define the bottom border for a specified element.
border-bottom-color	Identifies the color of the bottom border.
border-bottom-style	Identifies the style of the bottom border.
border-bottom-width	Identifies the width of the bottom border.
border-color	Identifies the color of all borders for the specified element.
border-left	Used to define all of the properties associated with the left border.
border-left-color	Identifies the left border color.
border-left-style	Identifies the style of the left border.
border-left-width	Identifies the width of the left border.
border-right	Used to define all of the properties associated with the right border.

Table A.12: CSS Object Properties	
Property	**Description**
border-right-color	Identifies the right border color.
border-right-style	Identifies the style of the right border.
border-right-width	Identifies the width of the right border.
border-style	Used to define the style for all four borders in a single declaration.
border-top	Used to define all of the properties associated with the top border.
border-top-color	Identifies the top border color.
border-top-style	Identifies the style of the top border.
border-top-width	Identifies the width of the top border.
border-width	Used to define the style for all four borders in a single declaration.
color	Used to define the text color.
direction	Used to identify whether the text should be displayed right to left or left to right.
font	Allows user to define all of the properties for a font in one declaration.
font-family	A list of the font family names to be applied to an element in the order in which should be applied.
font-size	Defines the size of the font used with a specified element using defined constants or a specified size or percentage.
font-style	Used to define font styling using one of the constants, none, italic, or oblique.
font-variant	Defines whether or not to display text in a small-caps font or a normal font.
font-weight	Used to define the font weight using a constant value (normal, bold, bolder, lighter) or a numeric value from 100 to 900.
letter-spacing	This property is used to define the spacing between letters.
list-style	Used to set all of the list properties.
list-style-image	Defines an image file as the bullet for the list.
list-style-position	Used to define the location of the list marker. Possible values are inside and outside.
list-style-type	Defines the type of marker displayed with the list.
margin	Used to set all margins in a single definition.
margin-bottom	Used to define the bottom margin.

Table A.12: CSS Object Properties

Property	Description
margin-left	Used to define the left margin.
margin-right	Used to define the right margin.
margin-top	Used to define the top margin.
text-align	This value identifies the how the text should be aligned relative to the element.
text-decoration	Used to define special text attributes, such as underlined or strike-through.
text-indent	This property allows user to define indentation for the first text line in an element.
text-transform	This allows user to transform the case of the supplied text.
white-space	Used to define how white space within an element is handled relative to the text within the element.
word-spacing	This property is used to define the amount of spacing between words within an element.

Table A.13: CSS Border Styles

Value	Description
none	No border is displayed.
hidden	Achieves the same result as "none."
dotted	Displays a dotted line border.
dashed	Displays a dashed line border.
solid	Displays a solid line border.
double	Displays a double line border.
groove	A 3-D "grooved" border is displayed.
ridge	A "ridged" 3-D border is used.
inset	A border with an inset 3-D effect is displayed.
Outset	A border with an outset 3-D effect is displayed.

Table A.14: CSS Font Constants

Font Constant	Description
caption	Use the same font defined for captioned controls (radio buttons, drop downs, etc.).
icon	Use the same font used for text displayed with icons.
menu	Use the same font displayed on window menus.
message-box	Use the same font displayed within message boxes.
status-bar	Use the same font displayed within the window status bar.

Table A.15: CSS Font-size Constants

Font Size Constant	Description
xx-small	Double extra small.
x-small	Extra small fonts.
Small	Font's displayed in small point size.
Medium	Item is displayed using medium font size.
Large	Font displayed using the "large" font size based on the browsers font settings.
x-large	Font displayed using the "extra large" font size based on the browsers font settings.
xx-large	Font displayed using the double extra for double extra large font ize based on the browsers font settings.
smaller	Displays the font one font size smaller than the current setting in effect.
larger	The font is shown in one point size larger than the current setting in effect.

Table A.16: CSS List Style Type Values

List Style Type	Description
none	No list marker is displayed.
disc	A filled circle (disc) is displayed.
circle	An open circle is displayed.
square	A square marker is displayed.
decimal	Numeric markers are displayed.
decimal-leading-zero	Numeric markers with leading zeros are displayed.
lower-roman	Lower case roman numerals are displayed.
upper-roman	Upper case roman numerals are displayed.
lower-alpha	Lower case letters are used for markers (a,b,c).
upper-alpha	Upper case letters are used for markers (A, B, C).

Table A.17: CSS text-decoration Property Values.

Value	Description
blink	The text blinks when displayed.
line-through	The text is displayed in a strikethrough style.
none	No decoration is applied.
overline	A line is displayed above the text.
underline	A line is displayed under the text.

Index